School Leaders
Building Capacity
From Within

School Leaders Building Capacity

From Within

Resolving Competing Agendas Creatively

Leonard C. Burrello
Lauren P. Hoffman
Foreword by Robert Fritz
Lynn E. Murray

CORWIN PRESS
A Sage Publications Company
Thousand Oaks, California

For information:

Corwin Press
A Sage Publications Company
2455 Teller Road
Thousand Oaks, California 91320
www.corwinpress.com

Sage Publications Ltd.
1 Oliver's Yard
55 City Road
London EC1Y 1SP
United Kingdom

Sage Publications India Pvt. Ltd.
B-42, Panchsheel Enclave
Post Box 4109
New Delhi 110 017 India

Printed in the United States of America

Library of Congress Cataloging-in-Publication Data

Burrello, Leonard C., 1942-
School leaders building capacity from within : resolving competing agendas creatively / by Leonard C. Burrello, Lauren P. Hoffman, and Lynn E. Murray.
    p. cm.
Includes bibliographical references and index.
ISBN 0-7619-3169-4 (cloth)—ISBN 0-7619-3170-8 (pbk.)
    1. School improvement programs—United States—Case studies. 2. Educational leadership—United States—Case studies. I. Hoffman, Lauren. II. Murray, Lynn E. III. Title.
LB2822.82.B87 2005
371.2—dc22   2004013789

This book is printed on acid-free paper.

04   05   06   07   08   10   9   8   7   6   5   4   3   2   1

Acquisitions Editor:	Elizabeth Brenkus
Editorial Assistant:	Candice Ling
Production Editor:	Julia Parnell
Copy Editor:	Stacey Shimizu
Typesetter/Designer:	C&M Digitals (P) Ltd.
Proofreader:	Theresa Kay
Indexer:	Pamela Van Huss
Cover Designer:	Lisa Miller

Contents

Foreword

If you are a teacher, a school administrator, a school board member, or a parent, we hope that you will find beneficial insights, strategies, and principles in this book to help guide your educational system to realize its highest potential.

What is the highest potential any educational system can expect? In other words, what is the purpose of education, particularly public education? (While the authors hope this book will be just as useful to those who work in private education, they are writing it from a public educational point of view.) Popular focuses for education have been to raise good citizens or to prepare a workforce. Some think that education can prevent social chaos and anarchy or lower crime rates and the spread of diseases. These are good goals, indeed, and any one of them justifies the investment a society makes in public education. But there is one goal that perhaps rises above all others: to enable each individual to learn how to create the life he or she would like to create.

If we focus education toward that result, we certainly will be able to produce good citizens, an exceptional workforce, order and well-being in society, and healthier—and perhaps even happier—people. But it will do several things more as well. It will put students in a unique position of being responsible; that is to say, it will encourage students to take the direction of the lives they lead in their own hands. The more they are able to learn to be the prime builder of their own lives, the more education takes on the role of essential ally rather than unintentional and intrusive adversary.

When the prime goal of education is to enable students to create the lives they want, students engage more deeply in the process as active, self-generated learners, rather than simply comply to a situation in which they experience little choice. Profound questions of motivation are answered by the true and personal aspirations of each student, rather than by conformity to social norms or reactions against the threat of a repressive life based on lack of education.

STUDENTS' DECISION-MAKING PROCESS

Our young people face many threats in the modern world, such as drug abuse, destructive sexual behavior, eating disorders, and various reactive patterns. These aspects of their lives are subject to the individual choices of each student, no matter what good sense we try to make them understand. We can't lock them up, control their every move, or monitor their interactions with their peer group—nor do we want to. We want to protect our young people from harm, but so much of their health and well-being depends on the decisions *they* make.

On a defensive level, we warn them against smoking, drugs, alcohol, sex, poor diet, reckless driving, and so on. But the best we can do on this front is to inspire fear about the negative consequences of poor choices. If the fear is high enough, perhaps they won't fall into the traps we, as adults, can see they face.

Conflict, pressure, and fear of negative consequences have a limited shelf life. The "sky is falling" warnings soon seem less compelling. Other immediate attractions seem to take on the glamour of forbidden fruit, even as adults' credibility fades. Adults soon seem not to know or understand how things *really* are, and the new authorities that can be trusted are other adolescents.

This is why part of education must be real lessons in how to make decisions in one's best interest. We need to teach our young people how to make decisions from the point of view of their long-term aspirations, rather than from their short-term appetites and impulses.

Making Good Decisions Leads to Success in Schoolwork

As students learn how to think about building the future they want, they also learn how to make critical secondary choices that support their longer-range ambitions. They learn that they must often engage in activities they don't particularly like, that they find difficult, challenging, frustrating, and boring, in order to reach their ultimate goal. They learn how to deepen true self-discipline and they come to see that learning is an important dimension to the life-building process in which they are engaged. They are then motivated to accomplish their homework assignments as part of the overall strategy that will lead them to their personal goals.

We also want students to learn to be objective about reality, learn the skill of critical thinking, be able to focus on desired outcomes, and be able to develop intellectual and physical stamina. The question is, can we *enroll* them in this cause so it becomes their wish as much as our wish? The answer is yes. We do this by focusing education toward enabling them to learn how to create the lives *they* want.

Is education set up for this job? Yes and No. The potential is there, but we, as educators, have to do our work in systems and structures that are not constructed for success. The cards are stacked against us in many basic ways. As we explore just how our educational systems work, we must understand that it wasn't anyone's fault that we have what we have. No one set out to design how politics, funding, training, leadership, unions, standards, parents, and students come together in a mix that often seems destined to bring out the worst in all of us. No one, with malice and forethought, decided to plot against us. But if they had, they couldn't have done a better job of taking the resources we have, blending them with dedicated, well-meaning, and talented people, to create dynamics that often neutralize success, produce factions, cycle fads, and make things harder than they ought to be.

The situation many of us face is more an outcome of systems self-organizing into fragmentation than it is of a lack of good will, good ideas, good people, and good intentions. There is plenty of good will and intentions, plenty of talent and innovative ideas, but somehow, no matter how good the people, the fragmentation works to grind them down. And when people do succeed, it is often by working much harder than they should have had to work. Success came from overcoming forces that were design flaws in the structure.

What can be done? After years of trying to intervene, people become rightfully frustrated, cynical, and unwilling to even think about school change. They have seen changes come and go and not lead to the promised results. They have seen people form into camps of dogma, assured that their position is the correct one and that if only everyone did it their way success would finally prevail. They have seen a pattern of oscillation—a predictable movement from centralizing to decentralizing, and then back; from local control to state or federal control, and then back; from traditional approaches to new approaches, and then back. They have seen that what goes around comes around. Change efforts often lead to lack of real change.

It is easy for us to become convinced that there is something unchangeable in our school systems. And even though many school systems have created exceptional results, real accomplishment, and significant advances, these triumphs lose something in the translation when the very same approaches are exported to other towns, cities, or states. This too-common experience directs our attention to a principle of nature: Success doesn't always succeed. In fact, sometimes success is systematically neutralized, even within the school system that originated it. For those who have worked hard to innovate, to find new and powerful approaches, they can begin to feel as if the gods are against them or that they are confronting a sinister dimension of human nature.

STRUCTURAL DYNAMICS

The actual situation is less ominous than that. It is a matter of *structural dynamics*. Structural dynamics is the study of how structures work—how elements within a system affect each other. Like its close cousin *systems dynamics*, structural dynamics considers the broader set of relationships that determine how a system behaves. The insight that both studies have in common is that the ultimate behavior is a product of the system or structure, and that without changing the fundamental relationship among elements real change is unlikely. System dynamics is especially good at tracking complex systems, but it is not often a good design tool. Through system dynamics we can get profound insights that can lead to useful dialogue. We can realize that things often are not what they appear to be and that our knee-jerk reactions to problems often lead us to solutions that do more harm than good.

System dynamics is a wonderful discipline that can help people rethink their basic assumptions.

Structural dynamics, while tracking different sets of relationships than does system dynamics, also understands how elements combine to produce predictable patterns of behavior. It also understands that any change effort, no matter how good it is on its own, cannot succeed when imposed on an inadequate structure. The reason why many good innovations in education have failed is that the structures in place rejected the change, as a body will reject an improperly matched implanted organ. Without a change of structure, any change effort, no matter how useful, innovated, or successful in other systems, is doomed to failure. What we learn from structural dynamics is how to support change by redesigning structures. It is a very good design tool, especially in education.

Structures produce predictable patterns of behavior. Some structures produce patterns of oscillation, some produce advancement. The telltale sign of an oscillating structure is that success is followed by reversals and then by a return to the original situation. An advancing structure is one in which goals are achieved and, instead of a reversal that neutralizes the progress that was made, the success becomes a platform for future success. When we are in an advancing structure, we are able to build momentum that makes it easier for us to expand, grow, and achieve our goals.

For change to succeed ultimately, it must be supported by the structure within which it is made. Many of the suggestions the authors Burrello, Hoffman, and Murray offer in this book are to be viewed from the vantage point of how can they work within our *actual* structures. We can't assume that good ideas and practices are good suggestions. For us to make ideas work they must be thought of from the perspective of a greater strategy . . . one that takes into account the actual structural dynamics that are in play. Sometimes, we will need to change the structural dynamics to accomplish our goals. This is a task that is impossible if we are unaware of current structures. Burrello, Hoffman, and Murray explore how to think about the structural forces in play and how we might redesign them as needed.

Some change can happen within the "trenches" by an individual teacher in relationship to his or her classes or by a principal in relation to his or her teachers. Burrello, Hoffman, and Murray give suggestions about how individuals can work within a structure that is unlikely to change.

However, some changes need to be engineered by groups of people. When an entire educational system takes on the job of redesigning the prevailing structures, those involved have a great chance of accomplishing significant, lasting, and dynamic change. Changes of structure lead to changes of possibilities. What was once only a hope or a dream can become a practical reality. But for this to happen, educational systems must move from chronic fragmentation to careful composition.

Fragmented educational systems self-organize into various conflicts of interests, structural conflicts, reactive modes, organizational and intellectual clutter, and predictable oscillating patterns. As the authors address structural change in this book, they explore how to build a system that can reinforce the goals and actions people take, build competency over time, increase organizational and systemic learning, bring out the best in people, and create momentum.

The more we as educators understand the elements of the structures we are in and how those elements combine, the less likely we are to villainize various elements when we are in fragmented systems. The more we can understand how and why fragmented systems operate the way they do, the more we can address the real impediments to success. We can become designers and architects of the structures, rather than simply pawns in a game we haven't made. The experience moves from being one that seems somehow conspiratorial to one that seems collegial.

LEADERSHIP

Leadership, as it is thought of in this book, is not simply getting out in front and setting direction for the cause. The leader is also an architect, designing new structures in which true progress can become a platform for future success.

As leaders, we must come to understand the dynamics we confront. As leaders, our designs need to establish a true foundation on which we can build. We need to have a compelling vision, and this vision needs to be shared. But we also need to share in our understanding of reality as it is and as it changes. This is not easy. It takes discipline. It is not natural for people to join together to study reality objectively and critically. But all disciplines are unnatural. That's why they are disciplines.

As we lead, we begin to build communities. The need for shared vision and shared understanding of reality becomes even more crucial to moving forward. And from knowing the desired state in relationship to the actual state, we can invent effective strategies and tactics that will enable us to reach our goals. We can learn to learn from our successes and mistakes. We can evaluate and adjust our actions in a dynamic feedback system. Together, we can grow, learn, accomplish, and build.

THE DEEPER CAUSE

One of this book's major goals is to help the reader reconnect with the deeper source of his or her inspiration, aspirations, and values in education. For those of you who have become cynical over the years as you have tried, but failed, to have the impact on education you wanted, remember—a cynic is someone who once cared deeply but was then disappointed. The question of how can this approach be different from what you've read before, tried before, seen before, is a good question. I think the book will clearly answer that question.

If there is an enemy in education, it is mindlessness. How do we become mindless? We think we know all the answers, and so we don't ask the right questions. We substitute our own concepts for true observation. We form conclusions and then impose our interpretations on the world. We generalize rather than look at the world freshly. We presume to know rather than not to know. We view reality from only one perspective rather than shifting vantage points to broaden our perspective. We drown in slogans, clichés, fads, and jargon.

Mindfulness is our ally. We need to rethink what we think we know. We need to ask authentic questions without a bias. We need to look from new vantage points, from broader perspectives, from greater heights, and with new eyes. And when we do, we will find something new. We think that education is a profoundly worthy cause and a noble profession. We think that it is one of the most powerful building blocks of our society. We think that educators need the right tools, understanding, and support to do their jobs. This book seeks to be an aid in that cause.

Robert Fritz

Preface

The purpose of this book is to help school leaders and teacher-leaders to use structural dynamics to improve teaching and learning in schools and classrooms. We decided to write this book because we believe a single school leader alone cannot increase school capacity to serve all learners using traditional planning and management strategies. With an understanding of structural dynamics, leaders can help to keep their schools from oscillating between the structural conflicts that divert them from where they want to go.

This book is for practicing and aspiring school leaders and teacher-leaders who want to create schools that are effective for all students. There is no doubt that during the past several decades, the context surrounding schools has become significantly more complex. Initially, school districts were more concerned with monitoring inputs and the cosmetics of the school plant and classrooms. With an increasing complexity and dissatisfaction with many aspects of schooling, school districts began to monitor educational processes, including such things as lesson plans, classroom management, and the completion of required school accreditation and self-studies. This internal monitoring was largely activity-oriented, with little attention paid to student results. This has evolved now to federal and state governments monitoring schools from the outside by measuring student performance using normative assessments.

The current era of accountability has clearly created a need for the school principal to acquire new knowledge, skills, and dispositions and to assume new roles and responsibilities. Principals need to expand their focus to include not only school management but also instructional leadership, which includes knowing how to create schools that produce success for all students. This requires them to understand the purpose of their leadership and how that affects their everyday work with staff, students, and families. They must establish a moral purpose, with guiding principles to direct and focus their work. They also need to work with the school community, create a democratic community, and build instruction program coherence in their school. This is complex work, and it requires not only commitment and ongoing learning but also a planning strategy to know how to put these structures in place.

The design strategy at the foundation of our work is driven by Robert Fritz's theory of structural dynamics and his concepts of structural tension and structural conflict, outlined in his book *The Path of Least Resistance for Managers* (1999). We chose this design strategy because it allows us to create what matters, has an outcome orientation, and is dynamic. It starts with creating what matters to a school community, providing an opportunity to bring into being, for example, personalized learning for all students. What you want to create is translated into measurable end results. This outcome orientation is fundamental to the current context of school accountability. It's dynamic in that school teams can continuously assess the tension between desired end results and the status quo. It allows school leaders to adjust to and accommodate the changes happening weekly in their schools. Finally, structural conflict is an equally important concept to consider because it helps us examine what structures are preventing movement toward our desired end results.

This book is organized into three distinct but interrelated segments. The first section contains the stories of three leaders, their faculty, and community members providing a running context for the book. In Chapter 1, we outline the context, action, and motivation to change that we found in three schools. We selected these three stories because they are examples of schools in transformation that have achieved excellent results. In the remaining chapters of the book, we return to the stories to illustrate the principles of structural dynamics and the essential elements emphasized in each chapter.

In the second section, composed of Chapters 2 and 3, we introduce Fritz's (1999) foundational principles of structural dynamics. We offer key definitions and illustrations to help explain the concepts of *structural tension* and *structural conflict* as applied in organizations—and especially in schools. We explain why your schools oscillate and experience structural conflict, and we offer a model for advancing toward your goals.

In the third section, Chapters 4–7, we bring together what we believe to be the four key elements required to move schools forward: moral purpose and principles, community building, instructional program coherence, and leadership. We offer illustrations of those principles and elements in action through the stories of our leaders in their schools. We attempt to show how the principles of structural dynamics interplay both with these important transformative elements and within our stories.

The leaders you encounter in this book are drawn from the teaching staff and community of parents in each of these schools. Together, they transformed their schools into more personalized and communal settings that made everyone count and be accountable for student learning. Their results demonstrate their success. Our hope is that you come to know how to use Robert Fritz's concepts and our application of his work to yours. Good luck.

Acknowledgments

The authors would like to acknowledge the work of school leaders in their districts and in schools throughout the country whom we have had the pleasure to serve and from whom we have learned so much.

For this book, the authors especially want to thank Robert Fritz, who provides us all with a way of thinking and acting to create the kind of schools we want for all students.

Leonard Burrello, Lauren Hoffman,
and Lynn Murray
September 2004

Corwin Press gratefully acknowledges the contributions of the following individuals:

Albert Armer
Principal
Wortham Elementary School
Wortham, Texas

Royce Avery
Principal
Woodsboro High School
Woodsboro, Texas

Bruce Barnett
Professor
Dept. of Educational
Leadership & Policy Studies
University of Texas, San Antonio
San Antonio, Texas

Scott Hollinger
2003 National Distinguished
Principal
McAuliffe Elementary School
McAllen, Texas

Michele Pecina
2003 National Distinguished
Principal
James Monroe Year-Round
Elementary
Madera, California

Phil Silsby
Principal
Belleville West High
School
Belleville, Illinois

Dana Trevethan
Principal
Turlock High School
Turlock, California

About the Authors

Leonard C. Burrello is professor of education, chair of the Educational Leadership Program, and executive director of *The Forum on Education* at Indiana University. He is currently studying school improvement in rural schools within a distributive leadership framework and consulting with the Gates Initiative on Small Schools for the University of Indianapolis in the Indianapolis Public Schools and teaches courses on moral and distributive leadership and organizational change at Indiana University.

With coauthor Lauren Hoffman, Dr. Burrello completed a three-organizational consultation project in Washtenaw County, Michigan, where they helped create a new planning framework using the work of Robert Fritz. They are also working with the Illinois Cooperative Leadership project to help build more learner-centered schools. His collaboration with coauthor Lynn Murray began in 1993 with a study of her leadership in a suburban district in Vermont. Dr. Burrello has consulted with both coauthors to build a new organizational structure and planning process in a large urban, midwestern school district.

Lauren P. Hoffman is assistant professor of education at Lewis University a visiting professor at Indiana University. She joined the Lewis University faculty after a 27-year career as a practicing speech and language specialist, supervisor, professional development specialist, and assistant director of special education in two large suburban Chicago cooperatives.

Dr. Hoffman codeveloped and codirects the TECnet project, which focuses school teams building unified systems to support all students. In addition, she consults with school districts and school teams on issues related to curriculum, instruction, and assessment and has applied her Fritz training in Michigan, Illinois, and Indiana school districts over the past four years. She has recently completed a new manual on *Linking IEPs to State Learning Standards* (2002) and has published an article with Professor Burrello in the *Education Administrative Quarterly*. Dr. Hoffman is currently helping to develop Lewis's new doctoral studies in leadership and is teaching courses on development and learning, instructional strategies, and performance-based assessment.

Lynn E. Murray is the principal investigator on an Instructional Leadership and Comprehensive School Reform project and the former codirector of the Vermont Teacher Quality Project, both housed at the Vermont Institutes in Montpelier, Vermont. She recently collaborated with her colleagues in the Teacher Quality Project in the publication of the *Vermont Field Guide to Educator Mentoring*. For the past 30 years, she has served as principal of both a large suburban K–8 elementary and middle school and a smaller rural elementary school; in addition, she has served as a director of special education, a Vermont state department consultant and grant writer, and professor of education and chair of teacher education at Trinity College in Burlington, Vermont.

Dr. Murray codeveloped and codirected the first Northeast Regional Resource Center, which served New England, New York, and Puerto Rico, and was a member of the research and development staff of the Northeast Regional Lab. She has studied intensively with Robert Fritz for the past three years and is an experienced trainer for his organization.

To all those practitioners who we continue to learn from and to those who continue the work.

CHAPTER ONE

Stories of School Transformation

W hy do some schools transform? Why do some schools sustain their transformation? Why do some schools know their purpose and direction? Why do some schools succeed with all students? Why do some schools have staff that learn and implement new practices? Why do some schools have actively involved parents and community members?

This book uses the dominant perspective of *structural dynamics* (Fritz, 1999) to answer these complex questions and "demystify" the transformation process. We begin by introducing you to three stories about schools that transformed. All three stories represent the work of principals who, using instinct, intuition, or talent, understood and applied the natural laws and principles of structural dynamics on a level of: They were not explicit about why they did what they did, but they all had a feel for the structures that were needed to transform their schools. Our purpose in this book is to make visible what they did in terms of structural dynamics so that you can learn and strategically apply the structural principles in order to create the type of schools you want.

We selected these three stories for several reasons. The stories illustrate the principles of structural dynamics at work. The stories take place in very different contexts, communities, and school levels. Finally, the focus of the work in these schools is very important. These schools are dealing with issues related to equity, social justice, and the learning of all students. They are examining and defining the school's purpose and fundamental principles. These people are serious about what they do and are bold in their expectations and standards.

We refer to the stories throughout the book to highlight various structural laws and principles. The names of the schools and principals have been changed, but the events and stories are all true. We know you will relate to many of the situations in these stories and hope you learn new ways to think about what is happening and to implement new responses within the perspective of structural dynamics. Each of the stories is organized into three sections: Context, Key Concepts and Actions, and Motivation for Change.

TRANSFORMING COUNTRY ELEMENTARY

Context

Country Elementary School is a public K–6 school of 350 students located in a rural county in a midwestern state. It is an old farming community where everyone appears to be related to everyone else. However, over the past 10 years, the school district has become home to a growing number of low-income and transient families with no roots in the community. By 2003–2004, approximately 50% of the school's students came from low-income families.

This student population began to attract the attention of the new principal and school faculty in 1993–1994. The 1994–1995 district data reflected the following:

- Country Elementary historically performed at the state average in language and math, but by 1995 failed to meet the state average.
- Student attendance was below the state average of 95%.
- Parent complaints were in excess of 140 per year.
- Suspensions and expulsions were consistently at 30 or more per year.

- Special education referral rates and placements were growing to the current rate of about 60 students with identified disabilities—or about 24% of the student body.

These issues were beginning to create stress among the staff. Principal Joy explains her observations:

> When you put these factors together, I started to see some very significant signs of stress. I could see and hear the staff turning staff meetings more into talk times to relieve the stress. It was so high that we would try to give it away anywhere we could. And sometimes we were very successful. Sometimes we could talk each other into believing it was someone else's responsibility, someone else's problem. The talk was repeated many days so that then we could go home and sleep at night and come back and start all over again. But you know what? It didn't make it any better. You know, no matter how much we gave away we started each day with the same concerns.

Today, Country Elementary is assisting the other schools in the district to implement instructional practices based upon Schlechty's (2002) Working-on-the-Work (WOW) framework. His 12 design qualities are at the heart of the school instructional model that is now being shared across the elementary schools in the district with similar success. Country Elementary went from the middle of the pack of 1,113 elementary schools to 22nd in the state. Table 1.1 displays Country Elementary's achievement data from 1998 through 2004.

Key Concepts and Actions

Ten years ago, the faculty and staff were clearly feeling ineffective in spite of working harder and longer each day getting more frustrated with themselves and the students. Instead of 10 photocopies in the morning and afternoon, the faculty prepared more direct instruction and doubled the seatwork to get the students to practice the skills they wanted the students to demonstrate. Doing more of the same was not working for them. They

Table 1.1   Country Elementary Enrollment and Student Achievement Compared to State Averages, 1998-2004

	1998-1999	1999-2000	2000-2001	2001-2002	2002-2003	2003-2004
Enrollment	318	339	312	323	321	348
Third Grade						
Passed, Free/Reduced Lunch	No data available	No data available	No data available	No data available	82.0%	88.0%
Passed, Special Education	No data available	No data available	No data available	No data available	No data available	75.0%
Meeting the Standard	60.8%	76.6%	63.3%	62.7%	86.0%	83.7%
State Average	58.7%	60.7%	56.9%	57.6%	77.1%	64.1%
Sixth Grade						
Passed, Free/Reduced Lunch	No data available	No data available	No data available	41.0%	67.0%	77.0%
Passed, Special Education	No data available	No data available	No data available	No data available	70.0%	56.0%
Meeting the Standard	51.4%	71.4%	62.2%	64.4%	77.1%	80.4%
State Average	51.2%	49.6%	47.9%	47.5%	60.1%	63.3%

were coming to the conclusion that the lower-income students "just couldn't learn what we wanted them to learn. And their parents did not care one way or another." Principal Joy recalled the following at a staff meeting:

> We were talking and someone said, "You know our expectations are just too high. We're making it so hard here, we need to lower our expectations and make it easier for success. So our students will do better—everyone will be happy and things won't be so difficult for us and them." And when we first heard that, everyone thought, "Gosh, you know that does sound good, that sounds so intriguing." We were just listening, but we weren't processing and one of the teachers stood up and said, "You know, when you think it's time to lower the bar, that's really the time to raise it."

The need to improve the quality of student learning combined with a faculty belief system that could envision what that looks like was their next step. In Principal Joy's words again:

> We started to develop what I would say would be a very common vision. We decided that we knew we couldn't hand pick our students and we didn't want to. We knew that we couldn't hand pick our parents and we didn't want to. But we knew the one thing that we could control would be the work that we gave to students. As we started reading and doing visitations and sharing, we also found out at the beginning that we didn't know how much we didn't know. And that was another big step forward for us in changing what happened, and when we finally knew that we had to change, we had that urgency, and with that urgency then we were ready to move on.

The faculty recognized that Principal Joy was not instituting a lot of changes when she arrived; however, she was observing the staff's frustration regarding the lack of student achievement. One of the early elementary teachers noted the following:

> [Principal] Joy kind of felt her way into it and let us become comfortable and let us help make a lot of the decisions and led

us towards change. She gave us the freedom not only to succeed but to fail also, and I think that's a strong concept because we learned so much from our failures.

Other teachers agreed:

We agree . . . what we always come back to is, it's okay to make a mistake. You know you do learn. . . . If you didn't learn anything from it and you didn't make any changes from your mistakes then that would be a problem.

Another teacher noted,

But also when we started making changes, she made us feel like we were part of that too, that we were part of the team that decided to make the changes . . . that she wasn't doing it all by herself and it was a team effort.

An upper elementary teacher continued, "I do know and I feel like what she was doing was building trust before anything was done to make changes."

The hallmark of this principal was building a risk-free environment that supported teachers who wanted to figure out a better way to improve their practices and impact student learning. The urgency to change was established in this dialogue with her staff. Creating a disposition about change was one of her early contributions to her school improvement effort.

Next, Principal Joy and the faculty studied and visited other schools and looked at three or four school reform models, including the Little Red Schoolhouse, Success for All, Accelerated Schools, and the 12 design qualities in Phil Schlechty's (2002) WOW framework. One of Schlechty's staff from the Center on Leadership in School Reform (CLSR) remarked about Country Elementary School, "The school faculty isn't walking into Chapter One of school reform."

Principal Joy indicated that the faculty had been soul searching for some time before they approached CLSR. She observed that the staff kept returning to the WOW framework. Finally, Principal Joy confronted the faculty and one teacher responded in the following way:

It makes sense—it's meat and potatoes. It fits our needs. We do not want a prescriptive program. We do not want someone coming in and giving us a checklist. We don't want them saying you have to buy this book. We don't want them to say we're going to come on site and evaluate you and this is how you're going to change. We are professionals and we want to have ownership for the framework and the work we need to do. We need a framework like WOW that will allow us to do the things that we need to do and it will also show us how to keep those design qualities and do it in a consistent disciplined way.

Principal Joy reflected on the rationale offered and indicated that, at first,

I wasn't too excited. Being a typical administrator with my neck on the line, I wanted the checklist. I wanted something that was concrete. I wanted it black and white. I wanted to know month to month where I was going to be, what I was going to be doing, who I'd be with—and that doesn't happen in this framework.

They worked pretty hard, and again and again they continued to support the WOW framework. However, Principal Joy was concerned that the little direction offered in the WOW framework would interfere with their advancement. She knew she needed a commitment from the faculty and staff, because this was not a district initiative; this was going to be a building-level initiative. In her own words, Principal Joy shares her concerns: "That's pretty high risk for a principal because, as most people know, if the building fails the principal fails, and that usually leads to a replacement. I had some concerns, some big concerns, and I told my teachers."

With the teachers' interest in WOW increasing and Principal Joy's sense of time running out, she created some minigrants for professional development. A consultant from CLSR provided an inservice on a bus as they traveled to a soccer game 60 miles away from the school. Everyone was treated to a great day of fun and laughter with their spouses. While the teachers deliberated with the CLSR consultant, they were waited on by students from the school.

After the trip, Principal Joy requested all of the teachers assess their level of commitment to the WOW framework. She explains the teachers' reaction:

> Eighty percent came back and said, "We understand this, we feel like we could do it, we're ready to commit." We had nothing in the negative range, but you know that was still a pretty big risk for a principal and I really wanted 100%. So I asked the teachers if I got a couple of floating subs and if I would arrange a day where every 45 minutes they could meet with a small group and one would be a facilitator. I would not be in the meetings. If they could get those final questions out that were keeping that 20% from really getting on board. And at the end of the day they came back and they said, "We're ready. We're ready to go."

Principal Joy and the team of teachers who asked to be in on the lead team (her trailblazers) secured a $50,000 grant from the state to work with CLSR. The school team people took off. They not only took off, but they became the advocates of the program. After school they would be talking to other teachers, using Dr. Schlechty's books (1997, 2002) to answer colleague questions, and sharing work samples and writing examples. "The first time you do it," they all said, "it's scary." They used their own work samples to help others generate ideas. Sometimes, they would just sit down with a teacher and say, "Let's just take one design quality and talk about it or write about it." They started backward mapping for some, but everyone was developing his or her own response at a different speed and in a different way—a way that was comfortable for him or her. Nothing was mandated: It wasn't as if on September 1 everyone had to show all the types of engagement with each design quality.

The CLSR consultant noted,

> It's a highly inclusive place, and everybody was always invited. The information, the concepts, the CLSR processes and protocols and practices were always laid out to everyone. But it was clear that different folks were going to need different levels of help and that was okay.

Principal Joy supported those who wanted to move forward and continued to invite others to become involved. She also found it necessary to confront some of the teachers who refused to get involved and gave them a timeline to demonstrate their participation. She learned while working with the CLSR about trailblazers, saboteurs, and a whole gamut in between. She really took a good look at her trailblazers and tried, as much as she could, not only to encourage, to cheerlead for them, but also to find ways to support them. If they were really stepping up to do something, to try something that hadn't been done before, she would find a resource they needed, even if there was not a budget for that resource. She became very creative with grants, working with businesses and eliciting parent support and support from the parent-teacher organization (PTO). Principal Joy tried to make the work environment as safe as possible for the teachers who were willing to express their support for the new ideas. She talked to the teachers frequently about risk taking and helped them understand how important it is to learn from one's own mistakes.

On the other end, the saboteurs were the ones that kept her awake at night. As a self-described reflective learner, Principal Joy learned not to react immediately to a negative situation. She learned to look at a problem situation, reflect on it, and then come back with a strategy. She kept saboteurs and their issues always job centered. She tried never to make the issue personal for herself or a staff member. She kept returning to the main questions: Are students learning what we want them to know and do? Is the work we are expecting students to do engaging? Does it motivate them to learn in ways they need to learn? In Principal Joy's words,

> We were able to work through some difficult times with some individuals. Some individuals had to be changed around. Some things had to change. I know it's a tough call. I had to make those hard calls, and sometimes that just has to happen. I think that by doing that, it not only helped me to keep my focus, it helped everyone else to keep their focus, too. Because they knew then that the bottom line is we had to keep the main thing the main thing.

During this time of the searching and discussing of the adoption of the CLSR framework, Principal Joy catalogued the staff beliefs and values that she saw driving their approaches to the changes. Again and again, working in a collaborative, collegial manner in the spring of her fifth year and after the start of WOW planning and implementation work, she started capturing those ideas. She was looking for a means to bind the faculty together through a set of working principles to guide their work, and as she did so she kept coming back to 10 ideas. When they came back that fall, she presented the list of these 10 ideas to the faculty in a random order. Principal Joy characterizes the faculty's reaction to the 10 ideas in the following way:

> It [the list] is my interpretation of what you have been telling me is important. They had a comfort level with them, and I said, "Well, you know this is high risk" again. "Let's do it this way." We took our teacher handbooks and we kept all the old guidelines, but we added the 10 givens for that year and we tried to work with both. At the end of the year, I knew that they were ready to let the old guidelines go. After that, everyone had a pretty high comfort level, so together we took out the old guidelines and we threw them away. And so now when we look at the 10 givens, we say, "This is the way we do business."

Clearly, another of Principal Joy's major priorities was to start early on to collect data on the many sources of issues and activities going on in the school. She asked herself, "What else could I look at besides just state test scores? What did I need to see?" She started tracking parent complaints, retentions, and suspensions, and at about this time Country Elementary started to see things happen. Once the implementation of the WOW work started, the staff noticed a drop in complaints and an increase in parent involvement and volunteer time. They also noticed a change in attendance at events such as back-to-school night and parent-teacher conferences. They were running close to 100% attendance at the conferences and, if for some reason a parent couldn't attend, the staff contacted the parents and attempted to rearrange the meeting time and communicated their continuing interest in meeting.

The CLSR representative notes that the staff of Country Elementary has

> paid very, very serious attention to a whole host of common and uncommon ways of measuring success and success with

youngsters, with community engagement, and so they have been a lesson for everyone and they share it widely about what should we be collecting here in the way of real artifacts and measures of what's going on. Staff engagement, student engagement, and the whole idea of having the data—the evidence pervades their teacher talk all the time. It is literally embedded in all their school improvement plans. The school has had an influence [both] inside the district [and] well beyond the district. It's a place that shares everything. The level of collegial work here is extraordinary and it's resulted in a great deal of success for other places.

The final major initiative of Country Elementary's administration and faculty was to find ways of gaining parental commitment to the parents' role in their child's education. Principal Joy and the staff knew they needed to raise the expectations of the family as well as of the students, especially for students from low-income families. The teachers needed parent support to make school important and to help in the reform itself by providing their time to volunteer in classrooms to support student learning. Faculty also knew that to be a state Four Star School with high-achieving students, student attendance was critical. Finally, the staff knew they had to bridge the gap between social classes in the school.

Initially, parent complaints were high and parent participation was limited. However, Principal Joy and her staff did not remain resigned to the common perception that these parents, like their children, had low expectations for learning and that school was a holding place until adolescence and a job after high school. When Principal Joy first arrived, parent complaints and student discipline were consuming her time. She looked to the faculty and asked, "Why?" So they started to look at their parent communication and interaction patterns. They went to parents and asked, "When and where can we meet and talk with you?" The parents responded and said, "At the Wal-Mart." It was a neutral place, where the power of the professional was reduced and the parents were not put in the position of feeling inadequate for not supporting their child's teacher and the school's work.

After a few attempts at finding new ways of involving parents, the staff of Country Elementary latched on to an idea of a back-to-school night where the faculty performed a skit making fun of themselves and the norms of school. Principal Joy then took over and talked to the parents alone while the faculty and students prepared a treat for the parents on the school grounds. She asked the parents to commit to just two things: to get their children to school each and every day and to review their homework. She encouraged the parents not to *do* the homework, but just to *review* it. She also invited the parents to come to school any time they wanted to see what was going on with their children. Following are the words of one of the school's parent volunteers, who spells out the change in attitude and the nature of the invitation the school offers parents:

> A parent is a child's first teacher. And when we bring our kids to here, we don't relinquish that role. We become part of a team and there's a real team feeling and that increases the comfort level. We'll hear teachers say, "What can we do to help your child? You know, a parent knows a child better then anybody else can know that child—how can we help?" When you have that level of communication, you get a much higher comfort level.
>
> I was encouraged to become a substitute because I worked well with students and there was a need in the school. We know the kids, the rules, and they aren't as disruptive. A lot of our children, especially children with learning disabilities, are negatively affected when there's disruption or change in the routine, and having somebody that they see almost every day, you know, makes that transition very easy for them.

Motivation for Change

The motivation to change Country Elementary into a school for all students can be traced back to Principal Joy's own child and her frustration with teachers who told her that her son could not learn because of dyslexia. She knew as a parent and educator that her son was bright and outgoing. She knew he was competent to learn and caring of others. She knew he needed alternative pathways to the usual visual and paper-and-pencil approaches to learning to read. She believed that the school needed to be ready to teach all students—not just those who come ready to learn what the teacher has decided is important and then in the manner that works for only about 60% of the student population.

Simply put, Principal Joy argued that each student had to be successful each day and that the faculty's job was to figure out how to achieve this. She would provide the time and resources for them to learn how, but they had to decide how to change their instruction to reach all the students of Country Elementary. She was committed to results, becoming the leading data collector and school data scribe, recording both quantitative and qualitative measures of student performance, parent involvement, and professional development of staff.

Principal Joy's other driving urge was for each parent to have high expectations for his or her child. Again, from her own personal experience as a parent and special educator, she knew that school people often made parents feel worse about their child's performance. Many parents of Country Elementary refused to enter the school because of their fear of ridicule and embarrassment. In Principal Joy's word's again,

> At parent-teacher conference time, I got to the point that some families had just refused to come. So, I just asked them why. One family, which had a number of children in this school, told me—they said, "You know we did not finish school and, when we went to school, school was not a good place for us to be. Now you want us to come back so you can tell us how we've also now failed as a parent." And I said that's not what we're going to do here. But, you know what? They didn't have enough trust to come and try it.

Now, the school attendance—at 98.5%—is above the state average of 95.5%, parents are attending almost 100% of their parent conferences, and there have been fewer than 20 parent complaints per year for the last three years.

The final urge that drove Principal Joy was a desire to lead her faculty to become their own best resources to one another. She wanted to see her teachers as risk takers and inventors of an enriching curriculum and engaging instruction. She supported teachers in scheduling an hour of collaboration time for grade levels and special educators four days each week.

TRANSFORMING BRIGHT LAKE SCHOOL

Context

In 1992, Bright Lake was a school of 650 students, Grades 1–8, organized into 10 multiage teams. It grew to 1,000 by 1997 and so a second K–4 school was opened. The original Bright Lake School remained a K–8 school with about 600 students in this growing suburban district located in New England. The Bright Lake community is filled with high-tech companies, light industry, big box stores, and a supportive professional class of employees. The school has primarily middle-class parents and is above average in academic achievement. All but one of the 50 students with individual educational plans (IEPs) were placed and served within the school environment.

When its new principal, Dr. Terry, arrived in 1992, she found a school board committed to multiage structures, teacher empowerment, and technology integration. The school board was student centered and committed to teaching an enriched curriculum that integrated technology into the classroom. The board empowered a team of four middle school teachers to design their image of "a new Mercury team" to push the "leading edge" toward technology integration and student-centered learning. The team of teachers was given the opportunity to re-create themselves in all ways based upon their beliefs about how a school should be.

These four pioneers, along with the supportive school board, launched a yearlong planning effort that resulted in an open-design learning environment attached to the old traditional school structure and culture. Two other Grade 1–4 houses were also a part of the redesigned space. While the rest of the school had fairly traditional box-like classroom spaces, the culture in the elementary school was not necessarily so traditional. The multiage and individualization traditions of the English primary school had strong and deep roots within the elementary grades. However, the "upper houses" (Grades 5–8) tended to look like young junior high schools, like so many other middle schools of that day and age.

The school board also appointed a full-time technology thinker and planner who worked with staff to design teacher and student tools to enhance their mutual and independent work and integration of technology. All teacher teams were organized into multiage "houses" made up of 4 teachers and 80–100 students spanning four grade levels. Dr. Terry inherited 8 houses with their teacher teams, some fully committed to the emergent ideas of student centeredness and technology integration, and a significant portion of traditional middle school teachers operating in a traditional school culture. They all were in teams, but many of the teachers in the upper houses behaved as soloists or worked in dyads within their groups of four without having bought into the school board's vision.

Dr. Terry describes what it was like when she first arrived on the job:

> The district's philosophy and vision was being implemented by the Mercury Team [during its second year in the new building addition]. The feeling was, first of all, that we have the vision of what it's supposed to look like, but we don't have the road map. We don't know exactly what the practices need to be and, perhaps most importantly, we don't know how to get there. We don't know what all the essential elements look like in practice; we could describe them in visionary ways and guiding-our-practices sorts of ways, but not in ways that we could say, "Here are the forms. Here's what it looks like. Here's what you do on Monday morning, and here's what you do on Tuesday."

The school's achievement profile is displayed in Tables 1.2–1.5.

Table 1.2   Bright Lake 2003 Achievement Data in English Language Arts, Grade 8—Percentage of Students Achieving at the Standard or Better

	Bright Lake	*District*	*State*
Reading for Understanding	73%	74%	62%
Reading Interpretation	48%	53%	36%
Writing Effectiveness	79%	79%	66%
Writing Conventions	68%	69%	52%

Table 1.3 Bright Lake 1999–2003 Achievement Data in English Language Arts, Grade 8—Percentage of Students Achieving at the Standard or Better

	1999	2000	2001	2002	2003
Reading for Understanding	80%	62%	67%	68%	73%
Reading Interpretation	62%	29%	48%	42%	48%
Writing Effectiveness	77%	66%	75%	69%	79%
Writing Conventions	69%	67%	64%	55%	68%

Table 1.4 Bright Lake 2003 Achievement Data in Mathematics, Grade 8—Percentage of Students Achieving at the Standard or Better

	Bright Lake	District	State
Skills	74%	79%	67%
Concepts	55%	60%	40%
Problem Solving	63%	64%	48%

Table 1.5 Bright Lake 1998–2003 Achievement Data in Mathematics, Grade 8—Percentage of Students Achieving at the Standard or Better

	1998	1999	2000	2001	2002	2003
Skills	64%	78%	71%	76%	82%	74%
Concepts	60%	49%	48%	46%	60%	55%
Problem Solving	36%	59%	54%	53%	62%	63%

Key Concepts and Actions

When Dr. Terry arrived, parents were concerned about the changes and did not understand what the teams were trying to correct. Dr. Terry decided not to force other teams to follow suit before the teachers had the necessary capacity. Instead of trying to spread the change further, as the board expected, she tried to slow things down, to focus on creating a professional learning community throughout the school, and to raise teacher and community understanding about the core values and guiding principles of the school. The staff were concerned about the expectations of both the school board and principal to implement this model.

One thing Dr. Terry felt it was important to do in her first year was to reexamine student-centered teaching and learning. She formed a Program Council, a governing body made up of representatives of all teams and all parts of the school, and spent most of her first year examining every word in the draft vision/mission statement. The Program Council reexamined this statement, wordsmithed it, argued about it, hassled it, and worked it through time after time until the entire thing was rewritten. Interestingly enough, not much of its real substance was changed. The original vision was pretty appropriate, and the Program Council was now in full support of the values and principles.

Dr. Terry was not surprised that the statement wasn't changed much, because it matched the picture that she had in her head before she ever found Bright Lake. There was a sense of rightness about it and the teachers also had the sense of rightness; it's just that they hadn't had any opportunity to dig in deeply and develop the common understanding they now had. Having developed a shared vision among themselves and with the school board, Dr. Terry and the staff shared it with various community groups, including the Parent Teacher Association (PTA), and at community forums.

After the first year, as the community controversy heated up, Dr. Terry realized that she needed a structure to organize and facilitate the community dialogue. She created the Families-as-Partners Council, a representative group of parents drawn from each of the houses that met once a month to consider the same issues of vision and direction as did the Program Council, but specifically from the community and parent perspective. The community conversations continued, along with the Program Council conversations, over the course of several years. The two councils met independently, with the principal as the glue binding the two together, systematically creating a coherent learning community committed to building practices that supported the vision and guiding principles of the school.

During the second year, the Mercury Team was running as fast as it could to continue to draw the road map and develop the infrastructure needed to implement a learner-centered, technology-enhanced model of teaching and learning. Instilling parent or consumer confidence became paramount. In year two, Dr. Terry invited two researchers to evaluate the work of the Mercury

Team. During the qualitative study, the parents identified a number of challenges. First, parents found the individualized planning formats to be long, confusing, complex, and filled with detail. They could not tell what was going on with their child's performance as the team moved from letter grades to extensive narratives. The parents wanted letter grades as a way to compare their children's performance with children from other schools. Dr. Terry recognized that parents needed to be involved in developing a progress-reporting system that provided them with the information they wanted about their children. Second, parents complained about the appearance of chaos when they observed in the Mercury Team's house. The team then developed new traffic patterns using their movable walls and storage cubbies in order to give the students clear physical boundaries to help them determine where they should be at any given time.

Then, Dr. Terry commissioned another survey of parents and learned that parents wanted more communication links to the classroom. The team responded with a concept of a Thursday Folder, which included outlines of units under study and examples of students' work and other exhibits. Parents were asked to review the folder Friday through Sunday and to return it to a team member Monday morning. Teachers then reviewed the parent comments, made any adjustments related to parent or student reflections on the previous week's work, and planned with the student for the coming week in individual weekly conferences.

The next major action step during this period of scaling up was to respond to the state's new standards. Dr. Terry was a leading contributor to the state framework and brought her expertise to the staff at Bright Lake. She saw the standards as a friend and an opportunity for school teams to focus their instruction and classroom assessment clearly in a common direction without sacrificing their commitment to student-centeredness. She also used the standards and the corresponding focus on assessment as a way to bring a degree of accountability to bear on her expectation that each team would build their capacity to eventually undertake the essential practices embodied in the vision and principles. She knew the data required by the state standards would demonstrate to teachers and community members that the new teaching practices were having a positive impact on student performance. This would bring credibility to those new practices that parents and the community were so nervous about.

Two continuing issues confronted Dr. Terry and the Program Council. One was supporting new teams with professional development resources (i.e., time and funds) to help them get on board with the student-centered vision and to begin instituting new teaching practices. The second issue was the scale-up rate. The board and superintendent had taken the position that every team had to begin to look just like Mercury Team at a rate of at least one team per year. This fueled the opposition's fear and put extra pressure on Mercury Team, which was still on a very steep learning curve, ironing out their newly created practices and procedures. With the Program Council, Dr. Terry instituted "a school of choice" plan, in which each house would write its own program description, describing the core values and education strategy or process, and then parents would be able to select the house they wanted their child to attend. This eventually led to an action-planning process, which served the school well on a number of fronts.

Finally, a major task for Dr. Terry was to implement her focus on assessment and an action-planning process driven by each team. Each team was asked to analyze data on their own students' performance and to design annual improvement plans, looking hard at their instructional strategies and processes. This assessment strategy, along with the school-of-choice policy, ultimately became the means for Dr. Terry to protect the pioneers on the Mercury Team. The data did show, in time, that the Mercury Team strategies were producing high student performance, a fact that effectively reduced the community and teacher resistance and paved the way for phasing out the more teacher-centered, separate curriculum and instructional processes employed by the more traditional teams. This action-planning process also began the internal accountability processes for *all* teams. Accountability began with expecting each team to describe their approach, instructional strategies, and curricular topics and structure. Over time, it evolved into a structured action-planning process in which every team was expected to show specific instructional approaches and improvements in student performance.

The ongoing building of assessment tools to measure student learning also measured the intellectual and affective skills embedded in the state standards. Dr. Terry inquired regularly about student performance and student performance measures. Her lasting contribution to the school as a whole was to help staff build action plans based on data. Their action plans were built upon state assessments, such as the New Standards Reference Exams, state Writing and Math Portfolios, and norm-referenced tests. The school's test scores continued to soar as staff made adjustments annually based upon student performance data.

As test scores continued to improve, teachers were concerned about their failure to assess what mattered most to them—the love of learning. The tests, however challenging, failed to capture the generative nature of their work, their student-centeredness, their commitment to a lifelong love of learning and to developing a sense of responsibility and ownership in their students. Dr. Terry explains, "The only way we're going to get [students] turned on is to invite them, to cause them to become engaged, and so we just continue to expose them to as much as we can."

Toward this end, the last tool she developed with the staff in her last year was a student investment rubric to measure student engagement. Her Program Council worked for the better part of a year, examining the state standards, reviewing model assessment tools focusing on engagement, responsibility, communicating, and persistence. Together, they used their own experience, their commitment to measure what mattered most to them (not just state academic assessments), and national models to build an assessment system to use across the system on a quarterly basis to assess students' "investment" in their own learning.

Motivation for Change

Clearly, the dynamic urge of Bright Lake School was embedded in its developing vision and its culture of technology-enhanced learner-centeredness: student voices, values, and personal visions leading to higher levels of student engagement and responsibility for their own learning. A parent once remarked, "My child has more self-confidence than I do. She is encouraged to do anything, be anything, she wants here."

Dr. Terry's urge was to see that student learning was tied to the standards, yet powerfully connected to students' interests and personal context. The guiding principle was for all students to learn what we want them to learn in ways that had deep meaning for them and really mattered to them. In addition, the battle cry was to "making learning the constant and time the variable." Also central to the Bright Lake vision was to see students gain increased self-confidence in and responsibility for their own learning. Dr. Terry explains,

> We don't give up on any kids. When you try to think about what kids don't make it, I guess I'd have to say no kids don't make it here. In the almost six years that I've been here, there have only been two students that we've had to finally set up an alternative placement for, and that was because of excessive violence to themselves and others. I guess that is about the only kind of child that I can imagine not making it here: It is one who would present a danger to himself or to others. We don't fail kids. We don't tell them they're not making it. They don't walk out of here thinking, "I was a dummy," or "I didn't make it," or "I have an F average."

Dr. Terry wanted to take learner-centered concepts to scale. To demonstrate the principles of learner-centeredness within standards-based reform is not only possible, but those principles are the primary vehicle for all students to delve deeply into higher-order thinking and learning. Clearly, Bright Lake transformed itself from a more traditional middle school to a distinct set of families of teachers, students, and parents that embraced a shared purpose and set of principles to guide their continuous learning. Bright Lake eventually got to scale because faculty, student, and parent engagement reached new levels of respect and came to trust in a model of learning that encouraged individual and group learning that set no ceiling. They truly unleashed the power of students to explore and discover what mattered most to them.

TRANSFORMING CITY HIGH

Context

City High is part of a major metropolitan center in the Midwest. The high school student population consists of 3,100 students, which is large even by urban-suburban standards. It is well-balanced in terms of its diversity: 59% Caucasian and 41% minority (36% African American, 4% Latino, 1% Asian). The free- and reduced-lunch population is 30% across all groups. The district will be a minority-majority district by the end of this decade.

In the past five years, the high school completed a major renovation to upgrade its classroom environments and integrate technology into the curriculum of the school. It has enjoyed a stable and supportive administration at both the district and school levels, including its counseling staff, for a number of years. In the county, City High students are achieving at the highest level as compared to all its urban and suburban neighbors. It attained this ranking over the past two years. City High has traditionally been among the top performing school for three decades as measured by SAT scores, community surveys, state assessments, and state overall rankings for each subgroup of its population. Each student subgroup in the school is at the highest level of achievement in the state (see Table 1.6).

In 1998, a tipping point occurred. According to Gladwell (2000),

> A tipping point is really the power of context. What really matters are little things. If you want to change beliefs and behavior of your staff, you need to create community around them, where these beliefs could be practical, expressed, and nurtured. (p. 173)

Principal John describes what occurred at City High in the following statement:

> I think the one event that crystallized the philosophy for us was when a few years ago one of our performing groups went downtown to put on a holiday show and the parents and the relatives were all there to watch and there were some students who were missing from the group: Students with disabilities who were being included in this program were left behind. I think what really struck us was that this is not the kind of access that we want for all kids at our school. So that was part of the event that really caught our attention and made us go back and look at what we were doing and how we were doing it and what was motivating our actions.

The outcome was the promotion of the universal access policy.

Table 1.6 State Assessment for City High by Subgroup, 1998-2003

	1989–1999	1999–2000	2000–2001	2001–2002	2002–2003	2002–2003 State Average
African American						
Language Arts	51%	51%	52%	50%	61%	38%
Math	26%	37%	43%	43%	56%	35%
Special Education						
Language Arts	31%	36%	24%	29%	25%	18%/28%
Math	27%	31%	28%	41%	33%	18%/35%
Free/Reduced Lunch						
Language Arts	—	—	—	42%	56%	48%
Math	—	—	—	48%	56%	47%
General Population						
Language Arts	76%	77%	76%	75%	84%	68%
Math	60%	68%	71%	74%	80%	68%

In addition to this change for students with disabilities, the district hired a new African American superintendent who had been the City High principal prior to Principal John. He and Principal John continued to examine the performance data for students in different racial and ethnic minority groups as compared to their Caucasian peers, and they concluded that the achievement gap at City High needed to receive the same attention they placed on any individual not achieving as expected. They fed back the data to the staff and asked them to start to experiment with alternatives for raising student achievement.

For the past five years, City High has been outperforming its neighbors in diverse urban communities. Principal John and his staff of 215 professionals, 43 instructional assistants, and 120 community volunteers credit their renewed commitment to expecting all students to perform at high levels in part to the creation of a Learning Center. The center, by accessing all the resources of the school's classrooms, provides a place where any student can receive tutorial help, practice test taking, and make up missed assignments. The school also created service-learning opportunities and student study groups. The faculty's persistent commitment to creating accessible curricula, providing differentiated instruction, using criterion-referenced examinations, and writing rubrics across the disciplines have been the keys to their success. The district is the only one in the county accepting tuition students from neighboring districts. Over 100 students per year choose to come to City High from outside the district, generating over $400,000 in tuition payments.

Key Concepts and Actions

The tipping point sparked by the choir snafu led Principal John to gather together all administrative and counseling staff to review what happened. The staff called the parents, and together they laid out their concept of universal access. Principal John explains this process:

> We stepped back and looked at whether it was the classroom or vocational education, work experience for students, extracurricular activities—whatever. We stepped back and said, "Now, how does any student access those opportunities?"

We wanted to have the same pathways, the same processes, and the same procedures applicable to all kids in our school. And so that's how we got started and that's how we sort of do, disseminate, and permeate that philosophy throughout our staff and our community.

When Principal John and his staff first looked at how they were educating all students to high levels, the academic arena and success in the classroom came to the top of their list of areas that needed to be addressed. They felt they needed one process and one procedure by which all kids could gain tutoring help and class-room support, regardless of what label they had or didn't have after their name or whether they were in advanced placement courses or remedial courses: The labels should, they believed, make no difference. They wanted a situation in which all students could receive the support services they needed to be successful. They started with a regular education arena in which they had various resource centers for special education, which was a real duplication of effort. Principal John suggested the following:

Let's put them [the resources] all together and let them work together on behalf of all kids, all the teachers teaching all kids. So that one room does not have a label on it that says, "Smart kids only," "Stupid kids only," "Left-handed kids only." It just says "Kids." And so all kids access that room.

All teachers and support staff work on behalf of all students in the Learning Center. They used it as a model to spread teaching resources into the classroom. The special education resource teachers became co-teachers in the four academic and elective areas. The teachers have been able to model the Learning Center concept throughout the building. Principal John explains,

I think if you were to ask the teachers in the classroom what they have found since we instituted this, [they would say] that along with the high expectations that we have for our students in the classroom, we now have a way to pro-vide the high levels of support that the students need to reach those expectations. And the teachers find that those students who routinely use the learning center come to class better prepared, more informed, and able to contribute to the class. That generates a lot of other positive things that go on in the classroom when more students understand what's going on and you can get into some discussion. Now, there's no reason for anyone not to meet those levels of expectations because we have the support in place for all kids. And that's been a tremendous positive impact on our classrooms.

At the same time that they created the Learning Center, Principal John and the faculty began to focus their full attention on curriculum, instruction, and assessment. Program coherence in this large comprehensive high school came mostly through a discipline- by-discipline study of state standards and their alignment across the disciplines of the school. Principal John made it perfectly clear that his department chairs were personally to see that the curriculum was aligned with state standards.

One excellent example of faculty collaboration across the curriculum was the staff selection of writing as a means of creating a focus on communication and language arts. They built a writing rubric through their inservice work and expected all teachers—not just the English teachers—to use it in their academic areas. Next, they took on algebra, eliminating all math classes below algebra. They provided students with a series of choices and asked teachers to experiment with different ways to support all students from double periods (sequenced together or separated each day) to a greater use of manipulatives, more pacing, and more direct and ongoing reinforcement of concepts to be learned.

Next, they built criterion-referenced assessments that all teachers in a discipline used. They required essay exams in every discipline and study groups for teachers and students to study test data. In Principal John's words, "Tests are two-way instruments: What did kids learn? And what did teachers learn about their teaching? Exams are for both teachers and students. Each should learn what happened and ask, 'Why?'"

Then, department chairpersons gathered staff and identified two things they would do differently the next time they taught that course. They surveyed staff and shared what worked for them. Continuous attention to data, continuous attention to what worked and what needed to be changed, and staff time to study and discuss findings were the heart and soul of their professional development activity—all focused on teaching and learning. The alignment of curriculum, instruction, and assessment was fundamental to their success and the principal and department chairs' highest priority in the school.

As the school's minority enrollment grew (the central office shares data monthly by subgroup with each school leader in the district), so did the achievement gap between White and Black students at City High, Principal John noted. He took the data to the staff two years ago and said, "It's unconscionable." He challenged the staff to consider a way to get minority students to take accelerated and eventually junior and senior high advanced placement courses. He wanted to create honor students. He felt that minority students needed to see their peers taking the toughest curriculum in the school and being successful in those courses.

So, last year, they selected a minority cohort of students—35 primarily African American boys and girls—and put them in selected homerooms with 10 teachers, providing the teachers with a common preparation period and lunchtime to collaborate and follow these students as a group across the curriculum. They also provided inservice sessions for the teachers examining belief systems, instructional strategies, and assessment literacy. The students were distributed in groups of five or six in selected classes and formed study groups to facilitate their success in a more challenging set of courses. In 2003–2004, Principal John selected 54 students and 10 new teachers to have the same experiences and deliberately included Latino students in this cohort. He intends to use this cohort format to scale up student learning and teacher instructional practices year by year. Table 1.7 highlights the success of the cohort in its first year as compared to the peer groups. He is also using a series of minority-oriented achievement grants to pay for students to take advance placement exams as often as they want.

City High has also built a ninth-grade orientation program called PantherQuest to introduce new students to the school. Upper-class students, under teacher supervision, run the program each July. Approximately two thirds of the incoming class participated in learning the traditions and history of the schools, as well

Table 1.7   Cohort Achievement Comparison at City High School

	Number of Students	Average GPA	Average Credits
Minority Cohort	35	3.22	6.37
PantherQuest Cohort	481	3.06	6.20
School Total	3,014	2.80	5.83

as its expectations, programs of study, learning resources, and facilities.

Motivation for Change

There are a number of dynamic urges that motivated the spirit of the leadership and staff at City High. Principal John's concept of universal access and his commitment to high expectations for all students are the driving forces to providing equity and quality instruction and support for all students. Principal John calculated the shift in the minority enrollment to majority in the next decade and believed that the school needed to reacculturate the students, faculty, and parents to believe that all students can achieve to high level if they are properly prepared. This fact, coupled with the current poor performance of minority students historically in the county and his own school, has made increasing minority student performance both a personal and a school mission. Principal John continues, along with his superintendent, to challenge the faculty and students directly with the achievement gap between student groups.

This urge, along with his 31-year association with the school, motivates him to maintain the school's tradition of success in the eyes of the staff and community. He related that for three decades City High has been considered the best large high school in the county. He is committed to continuing this into the fourth decade, and the City High faculty is committed to continuing to achieve at high levels. According to Principal John, the vision stays alive through the faculty and the ongoing development of its new and existing staff. His professional development commitment and budget are the keys to his success.

SUMMARY

As you see, all three stories demonstrate different aspects of transformational change. The purpose of the schools became more explicit and their guiding principles fundamentally changed. We use these stories throughout the remaining chapters to demonstrate different principles of structural dynamics. The next two chapters introduce you to this new way of thinking and acting.

CHAPTER TWO

Advancing a Model for Change

D id you ever wonder why some schools seem to produce real gains in student performance and just continue to get better and better? Do you know places where all the faculty chime in with pride about their vision for their school and talk with fervor about how their values and purposes play out with their students in their own classrooms and subject areas? At the same time, some other schools, having all the right words in their mission and purpose statements, seem to bump along with occasional promising practices supported by a single teacher or isolated group of true believers. While there are "pockets of excellence," those pockets never seem to galvanize the staff as a whole and professional development never quite makes it all the way to common practices that make a difference in all classrooms for all students.

Robert Fritz teaches us that people in organizations follow the path of least resistance created by the structures that are in place. He provides an excellent basic introduction to the principles of the path of least resistance and to structural dynamics in his book *The Path of Least Resistance for Managers* (1999). Though written from the perspective of the business world, this book has valuable principles that can be applied to schools. Schools showing ever-improving student performance trends have an improvement path created and maintained by structures, as do schools that seem to be stuck in patterns of low performance and low morale. All organizations are deeply influenced by their structures—structures that cause them to exhibit oscillating patterns or advancing patterns as the people in the organization go about their work.

Robert Fritz (1999) has made a lifelong study of structural dynamics—*"the study of how structure works within nature, within people, within personal relationships and within organizations"* (p. 8). If we study the structural dynamics at play within our schools, we can begin to understand and even predict how our organizations will behave now and in the future. With a deep understanding of what Fritz calls these "laws of structure," we can change our organizations to achieve the results we really want. If we don't understand these laws, our attempts at school improvement will, at best, produce only temporary results, and more often a number of other unintended negative consequences as well.

UNDERSTANDING STRUCTURE

Let's begin with a definition of structure. Fritz (1999) defines it as *"an entity made up of individual elements that impact one another by the relationships they form"* (p. 25). To understand structure, one must identify both the forces at play as well as the ways in which they relate to one another.

Picture a school group that wants to improve students' reading scores in the primary grades. To gain insight into how the primary reading structure is operating, we might do well to identify the most obvious elements to get us started in our examination. Key elements in the "primary grade reading structure" would probably include the following:

1. the curriculum expectations and materials available for reading in the primary grades

2. the teacher's instructional strategies (what the teacher knows how to do and how he or she does it)

3. the students' current levels of performance (every student's current level of performance, motivation, and background matters)

4. the time allotted to the reading instruction

Figure 2.1   The Relationship Between Key Elements in Teaching and
                  Learning

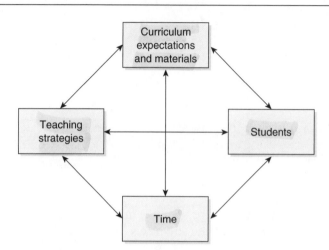

Once we've identified the elements, we then can take a close look
at how these elements are interacting with each other. We can see
the kind of "paths" they are forming, that influence teacher and
student behavior (see Figure 2.1).

An analysis of these relationships will raise questions (for best
results, think about specific students, specific curriculum expectations and materials, and specific teaching strategies):

- How do teaching strategies work with the curriculum
  expectations and materials? What strategies and materials
  are we using to teach to specific expectations?
- How much time does each student receive with what materials and what teaching strategies?
- How does each student respond to the teaching strategies
  and materials?
- How . . . ?

You get the idea of generating questions about the way the
different elements are interacting with each other.

Think the interactions through in terms of *all* of their possibilities. What happens when time is longer or shorter? What happens when certain students are absent? How does a particular

student respond when using instructional strategy *X*? When using instructional strategy *Y*? As you think through all of the relationships, you can begin to see patterns in the way the elements are interacting. These patterns are the *structure* of the primary reading program. The predictable ways that the structural elements interact *are* the primary reading program.

Advancing and Oscillating Structures

We gain insight into how our reading program is working by carefully examining all of the elements and how they relate to one another to form the "whole" of the reading program. Fritz (1999) leads us to understand that

> organizational structure is dynamic, and like anything dynamic, it is governed by laws. Organizations follow inescapable structural laws. They do so because they must. They have no choice about it because they have to follow the path of least resistance. . . . Any changes that do not take these laws into account are likely to fail, no matter how sincere we are or how good our values. . . . Organizations that take structural laws into account, when redesigning themselves are likely to succeed, because a change in the underlying structure of an organization changes the path of least resistance. Then energy tends to move most easily toward the successful accomplishment of our goals. (p. 15)

So we have Fritz's First Law of Organizational Structure: *"Organizations either oscillate or advance"* (p. 15).

Schools are organized primarily to advance or to oscillate. Schools that advance are able to move from where they are to where they want to be. Schools that oscillate find themselves moving toward where they want to be, but then moving back in the direction of the original position. Both types of schools might experience success from time to time; the difference is that the advancing school builds upon its successes—each success creates a platform for yet another stretch, another success. This creates a kind of momentum and energy that translates into long-lasting success.

An oscillating school, on the other hand, may experience success but is unable to build momentum with its individual successes, and so finds that over time it seems to slip back to where it started, no matter how sincere and diligent people are in their efforts. An oscillating organization might experience periods of advancement but will inevitably experience a reversal of progress. That's what happens with so many schools that we've seen "take on" total quality management practices, differentiated instruction, study groups, cooperative learning, professional learning communities, and so on. If the school doesn't address its underlying structure, if it remains an oscillating organization, it doesn't matter how good the intervention is that the school adopts—it will not result in overall systemic success unless the underlying structural pattern is addressed.

Structural Advancement

Fritz (1999) introduces us to the concept of *resolution* that happens as a result of our actions moving us forward from our current reality (our actual state) to our desired state (our goals and aspirations). The contrast between our current state and our desired state creates a tension that *resolves* once we accomplish our goals. This is an *advancing pattern or structure*: Something happens, something is created, and then something else is effectively built upon what was created.

For example, teachers plan for the first day of school. Then the students arrive, and teachers effectively use those carefully laid plans. Teachers deliver instruction based upon curriculum expectations, then they adjust their instructional strategies based upon students' midunit learning. They prepare progress reports at the end of the first marking period and then prepare for parent conferences. Then they have conversations with parents enlisting their support in their child's learning. Leaders and teachers examine their overall student performance data and then develop action plans for professional development and strategic changes to improve those scores. Principals coordinate all of these actions and weave them into a schoolwide road map for continuous improvement. When done well, the school's activities reinforce each other beautifully, leading to true alignment. That's the kind of school that consistently improves student performance. That's an advancing pattern or structure.

Fritz (1999) refers to advancing structures as the creative process, in which "something is created, and then, because it was created, it supports more and more future creations" (p. 17). In schools that are continuously improving, we see the creation of a collaborative learning community, in which everybody's work counts.

The staff of Country Elementary School created a forward momentum when they collectively agreed that they needed to raise expectations, not lower them. They agreed upon 10 key design qualities drawn from Schlechty's (2002) working-on-the-work framework. They developed a sense of urgency, an impetus to act as the trailblazers took on the trial-and-error process of developing exemplars in their classrooms to match the design qualities guiding their improvement processes. Principal Joy found the resources necessary to support their risk taking at the same time that she had the hard conversations necessary to move the resisters and quitters along or out. Each exemplar developed, each collaborative work session created something—and because it was created, it supported more and future creations. That's the nature of an advancing structure.

Contrast this with the early days of Country Elementary's story, when they were caught in a repetitive pattern of trying to give their problems away, blaming the parents and their changing demographics for falling student performance. Parents were not comfortable in the school; they did not have a good working relationship with the teachers and principal. Discipline problems were frequent, and suspension and expulsion incidents were on the rise as attendance was falling. This is not an unusual pattern for schools plagued with consistent low performance. In these circumstances, success is not building upon success. Isolation and blaming are the norms. The talents, energy, and wisdom of the teachers in the school go unrecognized and unappreciated. The school, as a whole, has no way to tap into these strengths to create any lasting forward movement in student achievement. Why? Because the school is behaving the only way it can in an oscillating structure. The structure creates impediments to teachers' best performance, and no one even understands why.

Structural Oscillation

Fritz (1999) explains that

the path of least resistance in structural oscillation moves from one place to another, but then moves back toward its original position. In an organization that oscillates, a period of advancement is followed by a reversal. Success and progress are nullified. The reversal within the structure is an inevitable product of the progress that came before it. (p. 18)

He illustrates the difference between oscillating and advancing structures with the metaphor of a rocking chair and a car. A rocking chair produces a predictable forward and backward motion, while a car produces a predictable forward motion, moving from one place to another.

Every educator wants his or her students to learn, and every educator wants his or her school to produce ever-improving student performance. But too often the schools are plagued with oscillating structures that keep pushing them back, limiting their successes, preventing the school as a whole to build any sort of momentum toward the improvements they want. School staff will offer a full range of explanations about why they have difficulties. The elementary teachers say the students are not coming in prepared to learn; the parents don't support the school enough. The middle school teachers say the elementary teachers are not sending the students prepared for the writing and math they need to do in middle school. The high school teachers blame the middle school teachers. Teachers bemoan their inability to overcome the social and moral deprivation of students living in poverty. Principals complain about the mediocre teachers they've inherited. Everyone complains about budget limitations. All of these explanations might in fact be true, but they are the symptoms, not the cause. Were we to ask what caused these symptoms, we might find some insight by looking at the oscillating structures in place.

This brings us to Fritz's (1999) Second Law of Organizational Structure: "*In organizations that oscillate, success is neutralized. In organizations that advance, success succeeds*" (p. 20). Neutralizing effects can take on different forms. Sometimes, success in one place causes trouble in another, like when we spend more time teaching literacy and so less time is available for teaching math and science. Sometimes, oscillation looks like success, and we celebrate it, whether it stays or not. This brings to mind the practice of having big community-building celebrations for special occasions, like we often see during the first days of the school year. We celebrate the community-building success of that one event, whether or not the long-term effects render a "better" community.

At other times, there can be time delays between oscillations, which we can only see if we step back and look at a period of years. This is the sort of thing that sparks district or departmental reorganizations every decade or so, or every time a new superintendent or commissioner is hired. Another reason why we don't see our oscillations easily is that we are in fact moving in the direction in which we want to move about half of the time—but we are still plagued by that "two steps forward, one and a half steps back" kind of feeling.

City High, until fairly recently, offered us an example of a fairly successful, but still oscillating, system. Until Principal John threw down the gauntlet two years ago, challenging that an unconscionable achievement gap still existed even though the school was performing above all other schools in its class, the school had been moving in the direction it wanted to some of the time for some of the kids. It was not, however, moving in the direction it wanted to *all* of the time for *all* of the kids. So, it was not yet building success upon success, but was still oscillating, still faltering in ways that were unacceptable to Principal John. When he challenged the faculty to develop ways to get minority students to take accelerated and advanced placement courses, he began to put an advancing system in place and take the oscillations out of the system.

This brings us to Fritz's (1999) Third Law of Organizational Structure: "*If the organization's structure remains unchanged, the organization's behavior will revert to its previous behavior*" (p. 23). In the City High example, Principal John wanted to foster minority honor students. To do that, he had to change the structure in which those students learned. He placed a cohort of students in selected homerooms with 10 specially trained teachers, whom he continued to support with ongoing training. He gave those teachers common preparation periods and lunch periods so that they would have time to collaborate and follow the cohort of students across the curriculum. He created study groups for those students to facilitate their success in their more challenging courses. He created achievement grants to pay for students to take advanced placement exams. These are all structural elements that Principal John put in place to enable his minority students to reach their goals. Without these structural changes, the organizations' behavior would surely have conspired, however unintentionally, to undercut these students' success.

We hope that you are beginning to see that the changes that we bring to schools in great hopes of school improvement are only a small part of deep change. We must look at the underlying structures of the schools into which we are bringing the changes. Let's take a look at Bright Lake School. If Dr. Terry had insisted that the change effort charge along with an accelerated schedule in spite of intense resistance, the organization would surely have been flung headlong into an intense oscillation that would have smothered the Mercury Team's fledgling efforts. Instead, the principal developed new structures, which allowed some decoupling of the houses, so each could create their own structures for a while. In the meantime, Dr. Terry worked with the school board and Program Council to further develop and refine the elements of the changes they were creating and to put accountability procedures into place for all teaching teams.

No matter how good any initiative or change may be, if the underlying structures of the organization remain utterly unchanged, behavioral changes required by the new initiatives will be short-lived. The behavioral changes will be unsustainable unless the underlying structures of the organization are realigned specifically to support those behavioral changes. In the Bright Lake case, the other teams were not ready to follow the lead of the trailblazing Mercury Team. Furthermore, the Mercury teachers were trying so many new things that their results were not error-free during that first year. To have required that all teams begin to look alike (which was the "typical" school structure, up until that point) would have ensured that Mercury Team advancements would have been reversed.

Instead, new structures were created. The school was transformed into a school of choice, where each team was able to articulate its unique philosophical orientation (within limits). This way, the Mercury Team was allowed to decouple and advance toward what those teachers wanted to create, and eventually to lead the entire school onto that same path (the path that was originally intended by the school board's master plan in the beginning). Over the course of four or five years, the Mercury Team and the school leadership were able to work in concert with the faculty and community to articulate a commonly understood vision and set of principles that everyone could support and enact comfortably and competently.

STRUCTURE CONTROLS ORGANIZATIONAL BEHAVIOR

You may think new ideas and belief systems are at the root of changes in behavior as we try to bring about improvements in schools. But Fritz (1999) teaches us that structural forces really exert the most powerful control on organizational behavior. For us to make our new teaching and learning strategies work in school, we must think about them from the perspective of a larger, deeper strategy that takes structural dynamics into account.

Fritz's Fourth Law of Organizational Structure tells us that *"a change of structure leads to a change of the organization's behavior"* (p. 25). We can have great goals. They can make sense. They can be the right learning standards, the right things for students to know and be able to do. We can have great learning strategies and scale-up strategies and still miss the mark if we don't think about the actual structural forces at play.

Let's look at City High School again as an example. They had a lot of the right "stuff" in place. They had attained high rankings over the years, with all of their student subgroups attaining near the top of their populations in the state. Yet they still found their student choir performing a holiday show that excluded students with disabilities. And they still found themselves with an "unconscionable" achievement gap between White, Black, and Latino students. They were using all of the best instructional practices with all of their students, they were the highest scoring school of its kind in the state—so why were these dysfunctional patterns still present?

They hadn't yet paid attention to the underlying structure. Their results began to improve dramatically when they restructured their delivery system so that special education and regular education systems were no longer separate. The Learning Center became a place for *all* students to use, not just students with disabilities. Tutorial services were connected to all students in all classes, from advanced placement courses to classes in the vocational track. Minority students were provided special study group supports to break down cultural expectations and to expand their possibilities for success. Support services were no longer used in separate settings but were "pushed in" to the classrooms. Special education resource teachers became co-teachers, no longer "pull-out" teachers. Writing became a requirement in every discipline, not just in Language Arts classes. Assessment became a two-way instrument, used to assess both student learning and the effectiveness of teaching, and was used as a planning tool to decide what to do next in service of student learning.

All of these strategies were structural in nature. The academic goals and instructional strategies were more or less already understood within the system, but they were more of a dream than a practical reality until City High educators joined together and engineered these far-reaching structural changes to support the academic goals and instructional strategies.

DESIGNING CHANGE INITIATIVES USING STRUCTURAL TENSION

We have seen how often change makers dive right into designing programs and new ideas before they really understand the forces at play. If changes need to involve groups of people to accomplish those changes, then they need to analyze their structures *first*, so that change makers can work with those insights to help redesign the organization so that a path of least resistance can be created, enabling the organization to create the results it really wants.

Developing Structural Tension

Structural tension is the most powerful force for organizing for change. Once you have a good idea for improvement, structural tension can be used to bring that idea into reality. It can be used to create what you want to bring into being. It is the difference between where you are right now and the desired or end result

Figure 2.2   Structural Tension

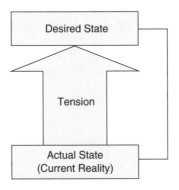

you have in mind—the goal, the big idea (see Figure 2.2). Fritz (1999) teaches that tension is "the difference between what we want and what we have—our desired state as compared to our actual state" (p. 29).

We can construct special tension. We can create a contrast. We can work with the difference between our desired state and our actual state. It is not a contrast of deficiency or limitation, but rather a contrast that opens up a path that leads to a plan of action. That tension, once established, leads to action steps that move us from where we are to where we want to be. Without the desired result or the current reality we have no tension. With both desired result and current reality clearly pictured and understood, we can move from tension to resolution. Energy moves where it is easiest for it to go. An especially well-designed tension-resolution system will sometimes be described as having a "sense of urgency," because people feel so compelled, their urge is so strong to get on with the actions that will move them toward the end result they have pictured.

Building Structural Tension Charts

To harness the power of structural tension, school staff members need to develop two abilities—for themselves and within collaborative groups—so that they can enact their school improvements and redesigns to open up possibilities for real systemic change:

1. They need to develop the ability to define clear end results.

2. They need to develop the ability to be objective about current reality in relation to the desired end results.

Fritz (1999) teaches people how to do this in his business and personal growth workshops using *structural tension charts*. We will briefly review the key elements of developing clear end results and current reality.

Developing Clear End Results

End results must be results you want to create. How do you know if you really want to create it if you can't picture it? You really must see it, form a mental picture of it. Too often, we accept vague descriptions of concepts as if they were the real thing. Would you know it if you saw it? You can't create something that you don't understand, that you can't picture. So, first and foremost, you must be able to picture the change you want before you can create it.

Is the end result something you really want to create or something that you want to go away? Too often, we develop goals that take action to make something go away—such as reducing discipline problems. Creating results means taking action to have something *come into being*, to bring important results (learning) into being. If you think of your end results from a problem-solving point of view, you only eliminate or avoid something rather than create and build something. So, this is important: Describe what you want to create rather than what you want to eliminate.

Use concrete outcomes (nouns), not just processes (verbs) with no outcome. For instance, it is not unusual to see schools gather significant school resources around teacher study groups. Although study groups seem like a worthwhile thing to create, one might do well to ask, Toward what end are they being created? Why are we forming these study groups? It seems likely that study groups might indeed be a structural strategy serving a much larger end that the school hasn't yet thought through. By themselves, study groups are simply a process goal, standing alone, and they are likely to have little impact, except to eat up precious resources and perpetuate an oscillating system.

So, for instance, the staff at Bright Lake School, while achieving quite well on the state assessment tests, was concerned about whether these tests might actually be distracting them from what mattered most to them—student responsibility and investment in their own learning. They developed an end result that looked something like this: "Develop and implement an assessment system that measures student investment in and responsibility for their own learning." They knew they really wanted it. For them, it was quite urgent, because it represented what they really cared about, and they were concerned that all of the emphasis on state testing was distracting their attention away from their key concern—creating student engagement and student responsibility.

They could picture the assessment system they wanted to create. They knew it could be a rubric. The end result wasn't about making something go away. They knew that if student investment was important to them, then they needed to create a way to assess it. They wanted to teach the community to value it as much as they valued the norm-referenced test scores. The change was about bringing a new assessment system into being. They were clear enough about what they wanted to create to move on to taking a hard look at their current reality.

Describing Current Reality

Once you have a clear, crisp description of your desired end result, you need a good description of your current reality using that end result as a reference point. Here, you need to think about what you know about the context and structures relevant to the desired end results. What resources are in place that can contribute to the effort? What best practices do you know about? What does research tell us about strategic action steps that are likely to help you reach your goals? What are the outcomes of actions already taken toward achieving the end result? What do you know? What don't you know? Almost always there will be things that you don't know. There will always be learning goals associated with important end results. What things are in place that can help you? What things are in place that can hurt you? Remember to look carefully at the structural forces in play. You are creating the easiest path for energy to flow along.

When describing current reality, there are some definite pitfalls to avoid. Seeing reality requires painstaking honesty. Just as we needed to beware of vague concepts when describing our end results, we need to be even more precise about accepting concepts, opinions, and speculations about reality at this stage of building structural tension charts. Often, when discussing current reality, people are driven to explain in great detail why or how current reality got the way it is, or to blame others for why it is the way it is. This doesn't matter. It's not really relevant. What *is* relevant is what the current reality is, not how it got that way or who is to blame. You want just the facts, not the editorials, not the clichés, not the speculations, concepts, or opinions.

Let's return to Bright Lake School and the staff's desire to build an assessment system to measure student investment and responsibility. Current testing approaches did not tap the dimensions of responsibility and investment in any observable or useful way. The community seemed to care only about norm-referenced, comparative test scores. Teachers knew that the state standards had many connections to student investment and responsibility. They could draw on that. They had rubric protocols upon which they could model their assessment structure. They had development time to do the work. Several teachers had stepped forward to provide lead writing and research to develop drafts. They had the full support of Dr. Terry. Not all teachers were as enthusiastic as the members of the Program Council, but there was a willingness to cooperate.

Figure 2.3 illustrates what this might look like using one of Fritz's (1999) structural tension charts. Without going into great detail, we hope you can see how the path for the Bright Lake teachers was pretty well carved out by the structural tension created by the desired end result and the current reality they described. From what they had, they were able to examine the standards closely, study the assessment tools and rubrics they already had available to them, and develop a rather sophisticated but economical set of rubrics for use on a quarterly basis to assess their students' growing development toward greater responsibility, exercise of good work habits, development of discipline and personal investment, and ability to express themselves and to work collaboratively.

[handwritten margin note: quarterly assessments to monitor student progress]

Figure 2.3   Structural Tension Chart

DESIRED END RESULT

Develop and implement an assessment system that measures student investment in and responsibility for their own learning.

[*This eventually evolved into a rubric they called the "Student Investment Rubric," which had components for student engagement; production, presentation, and evaluation; collaboration; and work habits.*]

ACTION STEPS

CURRENT REALITY

- Current testing does not tap the student responsibility or engagement.

- The community pays most attention to norm-referenced test scores.

- State standards for vital results do address student responsibility and engagement.

- We have good protocols for building rubrics to use as models.

- We have Program Council development time and teachers who are willing to develop drafts of the rubrics.

- We have principal support. She will provide the time and resources necessary to do the development of the tools and professional development required.

- Some teachers will need professional development to learn how to use the rubrics once they are developed.

ON THE IMPORTANCE OF
LINKING GOALS INTO A MASTER PLAN

If you want to effect schoolwide change, it is not enough to be able to construct and operate within structural tension on an individual and even small-group level. Schools are notoriously fragmented, quick to self-organize into various conflicts of interests, to get into reactive modes, to develop all kinds of organizational and intellectual clutter, and to sustain predictable oscillating patterns even while thinking they are creating action plans that work. Educators need to learn to think structurally and systemically.

That means you need to think about the nested levels within your system and align them. You need to think about a school master plan, team or section plans that are aligned with the master plan, classroom plans that are aligned with team or department plans, and student plans that are aligned with the classroom plans. You need to transfer the structural tension–charting tool to all the levels of the system and use them in alignment with one another. Then, the possibilities of bringing improvements to scale will become a reality. Goals and actions that people take then will begin to reinforce one another. Competencies will build over time; organizational and systemic learning will build and reinforce previous learning. Success in one part of the system will reinforce and create momentum for success in another part of the system. Graphically, this kind of aligned nesting of structural tension planning looks like Figure 2.4.

Again, we can turn to Bright Lake as an example. There, Dr. Terry established a schoolwide action-planning goal in key academic areas, in which each teaching team was then expected to develop a specific team action plan to carry out more specifically. Within each of the team plans, there were specific teacher professional development plans that were aligned, as well as specific student plans. Yes, even students made plans for themselves regarding how they were going to improve their learning performance in the key areas for improvement.

One caveat about the planning process and its alignment within the system: The plan is only as good as its *feedback loop.* The plan's current reality must constantly be refreshed. While we may hold our desired end result relatively stable (though it

Figure 2.4   Master Plan

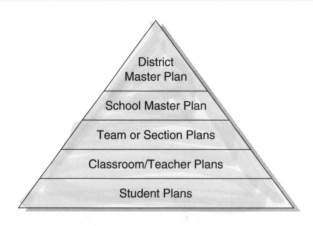

very Important

may become clearer and more developed the closer we get to it), our current reality will be constantly shifting if we are making any progress at all. Every time our current reality changes, that becomes feedback for our planning process, informing the action steps we are taking in service of our end result. If we don't pay attention to our current reality and constantly update our plans, we will find ourselves lost, having wandered off our charted path.

This failure to attend to feedback is the biggest pitfall of most planning processes we've seen. Failure to monitor is how plans end up on shelves gathering dust. No matter how carefully laid the plans, if they are not carefully monitored every step of the way, with constant updating, tension will be lost and you will find yourself slipping right back into old oscillating patterns. So don't take this step lightly. Be sure to reserve energy and resources for the kind of monitoring that will be required to keep you on your path.

PURPOSE AND PRINCIPLES
GUIDE THE ENTIRE DESIGN PROCESS

So far in this chapter we've talked about structural relationships within schools, about how people's behavior within organizations is controlled by the structures more than by their goals or even their values. We've talked about how to think about bringing the things we want to create into being and about how to align our efforts. But we haven't talked much about why to do these things—about the purpose and principles. Why do we exist as an organization? What is our profound or spiritual purpose?

Fritz (1999) encourages people not to spend too much energy wordsmithing and processing to try to capture their organizational purpose in writing. Rather, he suggests you spend your energy building your shared mental images through dialogue and deep conversation, by which you learn to recognize it. As he writes,

> We feel the purpose by what excites us, by the organization's true values and aspirations, and by the services and products that the organization generates. We also recognize the purpose by what disappoints us about the organization—its failure to live up to its values, the compromises it makes, its contradictions, and its inability to live up to it potential. (p. 151)

Fritz (1999) goes on to say about purpose, "We can feel it, sense it, intuit it, and align to it, but almost anything we say about it sounds dumb" (p. 152).

What's important is that you talk about purpose in your school, again and again. We offer a more detailed treatment of purpose in Chapter 4, but for now just remember that purpose isn't something that can necessarily be put into a tight little slogan or even a long paragraph. It's the essence of the organization though, and it answers the question, "Why do we exist as an organization?" It is important to take time as a school to engage in conversation about why we exist as a school. Too often, we take that for granted and lose sight of our essential mission. Without this reminder, our work can often become hollow and our attitudes can become cynical.

Graphically, our master plan model now takes on the shape shown in Figure 2.5. Notice how the purpose and principles touch every aspect of every plan. In this figure, you see that the purpose and principles drive the school master plan, which drives the team/section plans, which drives the classroom/teacher plans, which drives the students plans. Yet this is a reciprocal process. The student plans feed the classroom plans, which feed the team plans, which feed the school plans—all in service of the purpose and in accordance with the values and principles of the school.

Figure 2.5   Purpose and Principles + Master

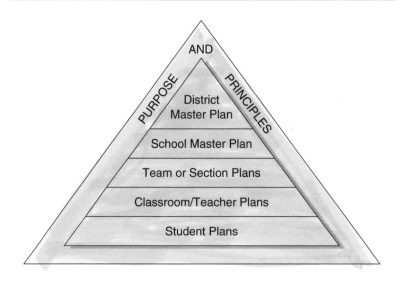

As we learn how to address structural change, we learn how to build a system that can reinforce and align the goals and actions that people take. We learn how to build structural tension to create the outcomes we want in accord with what matters most and in alignment with our most fundamental values and aspirations. We learn how to bring out the best in people by creating momentum born of advancing structures. At best, we can become designers and architects of the structures, rather than mice in a maze of structures oscillating in ways invisible and bewildering.

SUMMARY

In summary, here is a review Fritz's (1999) four Laws of Organizational Structure and a few tips for thinking structurally about change and planning for school transformation:

- Organizations either oscillate or advance (Fritz's First Law of Organizational Structure).
- In organizations that oscillate, success is neutralized. In organizations that advance, success succeeds (Fritz's Second Law of Organizational Structure).

- If the organization's structure remains unchanged, the organization's behavior will revert to its previous behavior (Fritz's Third Law of Organizational Structure).
- A change of structure leads to a change of the organization's behavior (Fritz's Fourth Law of Organizational Structure).
- In any change effort, analyze the structural elements in play around you and work with those elements to help redesign the organization so that the path of least resistance for what you are trying to create can be found.
- Structural tension is the most powerful force for organizational change. Once you know what you want to create, structural tension can be used to bring it into reality.
- Structural tension is created when you define clear end results and are objective about current reality in relation to those end results.
- You can create structural tension charts to help you plan within all levels of the system. Be sure to reserve time and resources for frequent checks on current reality. When you are in touch with your current reality, you build on the platforms of your success, gathering momentum as you go. If you don't check current reality, you don't know where you are!
- As you develop master plans (i.e., structural tension charts), think about the nested levels (district, school, departments, teams, classroom, student teams, individual students) within your system and align them. You need to transfer the structural tension–charting tool to all the levels of the system and use them in alignment with one another. Goals and actions that people take then will begin to reinforce one another. Success in one part of the system will reinforce and create momentum for success in another part of the system.
- Don't overlook purpose and principles that drive an organizational master plan. Be clear about why your school exists. Don't just take it for granted that everybody knows why. Take the time to revisit your deepest values now and again.

In the next chapter, we'll take a closer look at the nature of structural oscillation and how it creates insurmountable impediments to long-term success.

CHAPTER THREE

Understanding Structural Conflict

The More Things Change,
the More They Stay the Same

E ducators are well acquainted with the pendulum swings in education. In the past 30 years, we have seen schools change from a conservative 3Rs (reading, writing, and arithmetic) approach, to a progressive approach with looser curriculum and more student control, then back to the 3Rs again. We centralize, then decentralize, then centralize again. Administrators take control, making most of the decisions; then we turn to teacher-leaders, asking them to become highly involved in decision making, only to move back again to administrator-driven decision making. The primary grades were taught with the whole-language approach and then moved to the phonics approach as a better way to teach early reading, only to return to the whole-language approach, then back again to phonics—and the battle *still* rages.

We've seen school architecture swing from closed classrooms to open classrooms and back again. We've seen the full range of approaches to instruction, from a national curriculum to total individualization, to student-centered and determined curriculum, and now back again to a default national curriculum driven by national testing. Is it any wonder that people accuse schools of responding to the latest fad, while true believers think they are mounting an important change effort? Is it any wonder that change and school improvement efforts are not taken seriously by people inside or outside of the system? Instead, they think it's just one more thing that will fade away and be replaced by a new and equally short-lived fad or fury of tomorrow.

Worse yet, people polarize into camps at different points in the pendulum swing, pursuing irresolvable arguments regarding the best, most effective approach—whole language versus phonics; open classrooms versus closed classrooms; teacher-led decision making versus principal-driven decision making; a student-centered curriculum versus a centralized, state-sanctioned curriculum; and on and on.

Aside from the conflicts emerging around change efforts, we can see departments and interest groups competing for resources, group meeting and training time, and/or approval from the school board and the public. Special educators vie for IEP meeting times with classroom teachers and parents, while classroom teachers struggle for collegial and solo instructional planning time. Counselors and behavior specialists vie for time with teachers for training on discipline and effective behavior management, while the central office administrators vie for that very same time for training on blood-borne pathogens and confidentiality procedures. School schedules are built at the convenience of the "specialists" (e.g., physical education, art, music, etc.) or are built to provide shared planning time for core teaching teams.

These pendulum swings, special interest groups, and competition for scarce resources create oscillation. Attention oscillates from one approach to another and then back again. Or specific interest groups manage to gain the upper hand on resources, but only for a while, until some event or person shifts the priorities and power in another direction. Some believe there is no reasonable way that a school can respond to all the forces in play, all the demands for attention from so many different levels and interest groups. Educators attest more and more that they are bombarded day in and day out by a myriad of competing demands, new mandates, new rules and expectations—bringing with it a growing sense of being out of control, of "too much going on," and of feeling overwhelmed.

OSCILLATION—OR, WHO OR WHAT IS ON TOP TODAY

Robert Fritz (1999) explains in *The Path of Least Resistance for Managers* that this chronic oscillation is caused by structural conflicts within the organization: "While a simple tension-resolution system causes structural tension, structural conflict is produced by a more complex structure: two competing tension-resolution systems based on two completing goals" (p. 92). This is explained, simply, through a nonorganizational example: the dieting yo-yo so frequently experienced by people concerned about being overweight. We have two competing tension-resolution systems at play. First there is the tension of being hungry, which is resolved by eating (see Figure 3.1).

Figure 3.1   Eating Tension-Resolution System

But, if a person begins to weigh more than he or she would like to, he or she forms another tension-resolution system, to be resolved by going on a diet (see Figure 3.2).

Figure 3.2   Dieting Tension-Resolution System

Fritz (1999) explains, "As each system moves toward its own resolution, it competes with the conflicting system. First, the dominant, or most pronounced tension is hunger. In order to resolve that tension, we eat" (p. 93). Figure 3.3 shows the eating-dieting conflict.

"Once we have eaten, our hunger diminishes. But, unfortunately for most of us, our weight goes up. The amount we weigh is different from the amount we want to weight. This difference then becomes the more pronounced tension" (p. 93). See Figure 3.4 for an illustration of this tension.

Figure 3.3   Eating and Dieting—Conflicting Systems

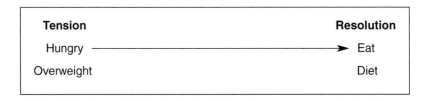

Figure 3.4   Eating Leads to Becoming Overweight

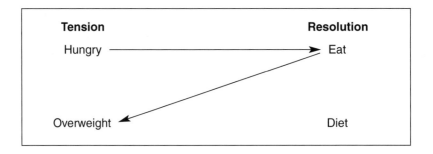

Figure 3.5   Dieting System Becomes Strongest

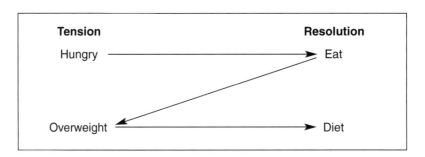

"In order to resolve this tension, we may eat less, or skip meals" (p. 93), thus the diet becomes dominant in the conflict, as illustrated in Figure 3.5.

"We may lose some pounds and we begin to feel better about our weight. But the body doesn't like this situation one bit and reacts to reduction of fat and protein by sending a starvation warning—'Eat! Eat! Eat!'" (p. 94). And so it goes. Most

Figure 3.6 Classic Dieting Oscillation—Structural Conflict

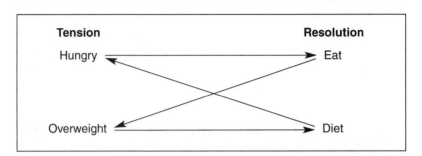

dieters eventually succumb to the appetite's outrage, which sends them back into the hunger tension-resolution system, where the path of least resistance is to eat, as illustrated in Figure 3.6.

As Fritz (1999) writes,

> This kind of movement between one tension-resolution system and its competing tension-resolution system is called a shift of dominance. A shift of dominance produces a predictable oscillating pattern, as the path of least resistance moves from one type of action (eating) to another (dieting). In our example, hunger leads to eating, which leads to weight gain, which leads to dieting, which leads to hunger, as the path of least resistance changes. (p. 94)

This same pattern of oscillation occurs within organizational systems, and of course schools are no exception. Thus we see the kind of pendulum swinging and polarization described in the introductory section of this chapter.

EDUCATION SYSTEMS ARE ORGANIZED FOR CONFLICT

Why are there so many failed initiatives? Why are so many innovations abandoned—or even worse, vilified? Is it because schools are not open to or capable of change or improvement? No. It's because schools are organized (one might even say optimized) for conflict, with oscillation on every front.

This oscillation is caused by the same structural conflict explained above. People are pursuing mutually exclusive, conflicting goals. These conflicting tension-resolution systems are the opposing ends of the pendulum swings. Schools are hopelessly burdened with too many goals—most of which create structural conflict everywhere you look.

Schools are organized and managed in ways that optimize opportunities for structural conflict. Schools and classrooms within schools are loosely connected, like little fiefdoms: classrooms not connected to neighboring classrooms, schools not connected to neighboring schools. Because they lack clear, overarching, organizing purposes and principles, they self-organize into competing parts, reacting first and foremost to their immediate context and short-term needs. Individuals tend to react and respond with short-sightedness, influenced by events and relationships that are right in front of their faces, with little thought toward long-term goals or the purposes and principles of their parent organization.

Why do they lack clear purposes and principles? Often, because there are so many of them, it is possible to find a purpose or principle for any possible decision or direction. Within this intellectual, philosophical, and organizational clutter, schools have so *many* purposes that they conflict with one another in a world of limited time and capacity. So, people are often left to their own devices simply to make short-term and immediate sense of their isolated environment and immediate relationships as they make important decisions about their students, instruction, and their learning.

Schools have many divided constituencies demanding that *their* priorities be top priority. Policy makers, school leaders, and teachers pretend to treat all priorities as equally important, trying to balance the competing concerns, trying to do justice to them all. But the fact is that they can't do justice to them all. Few months go by in a principal's life that he or she does not receive a new mandate reflecting some new purpose for schooling from the state department, the federal government, or the local community. There is the persistent cry to fix this or that from every corner of the school community.

Structural Conflict and Tension-Resolution Systems at Bright Lake

Let's look at the Bright Lake School improvement effort, for example. Their goal was to reinvent education so that it was student-centered yet standards-based and supported by integration of technology. The teachers on Mercury Team, the administration, and the school board wanted to change the "work" in Bright Lake. So, one tension-resolution system was set up for educational change around student-centered, standards-based, and technology-integrated instruction. This was no small change. It involved significant actions and commitment of all the educators at the school. All teams participated in training in working in teams, in the integration of technology, and in student-centered and standards-based instructional strategies and principles.

The task of retooling their day-to-day processes to actually implement these new ways of working with students required tremendous effort and commitment. It required fundamental shifts from teacher as deliverer of knowledge to teacher as manager of the learning environment and facilitator of learning. They were flying the plane while totally redesigning the wings and the propulsion system of the plane. No easy feat! At the same time, the school board was clarifying policies and principles in order to articulate the essence of these changes to the teachers and the community. This tension-resolution system might be diagrammed as shown in Figure 3.7.

It may come as no surprise that this change effort quickly met with challenges. The Mercury Team, a group of "true believers," was highly motivated to stay the course. The members were

[handwritten margin note: Lots of training needed to change]

Figure 3.7   Bright Lake Change Effort Tension-Resolution System

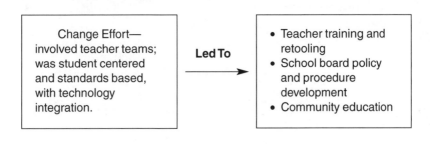

committed to a long-range effort to redesign the way they did their work, changing from a teacher-centered, activity-oriented, and paper-based instructional approach to a student-centered, standards-based, technology-integrated approach. There were four other teams in Bright Lake School who were not so committed. They were uncomfortable and unconvinced of the merits of the new approach. They were much more comfortable continuing the practices they had learned and believed successful in the past. The parents and community were also unsure of the merits of the new approach—in fact, they didn't understand it at all. It didn't look like the school they had attended; they had "done all right in life," hadn't they? The resistant teams helped to fuel the parent concern, transmitting their fear and doubt to their own parent constituencies. So, a conflicting tension-resolution system developed (see Figure 3.8). When you put these two tension-resolution systems together, you can see the conflict operating.

While there was resistance, doubt, criticism, and a counter-effort going on, the change effort was continuing. Shifts of dominance happened, depending upon when the school board had met or when a public forum criticizing the directions had occurred. Needless to say, forward progress was slow at this point, and confusion and anxiety were rampant.

The principal's solution was to move the system temporarily into a tolerable level of conflict while she tried to sort things out a bit. Though the Mercury Team remained committed to the hard work of retooling, the other Bright Lake teams needed much more training to build their capacity to the point that they could believe these strategies would actually work. Community members and parents needed a lot more information and confidence building. Furthermore, Dr. Terry believed that she would develop more commitment to and understanding of the new purposes and principles if she involved the teachers more in their development and articulation.

So, Dr. Terry began a yearlong process of articulation with the Program Council, a representative body of teachers from across all teams within the school. While this development work was continuing, the school board, Program Council, and administration decided that they would work within a school of "choice," in which parents could choose the approach they thought would work best for their child. So, the Mercury Team continued to develop its new structures while the other teams continued more

Figure 3.8   Change Effort Meets Resistance—Structural Conflict at Bright Lake

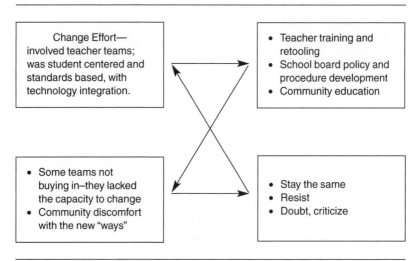

or less as they always had, though slowly adopting bits and pieces from the "new" way over the years that followed. After the initial structural conflict set itself up, it evolved into a slightly different pattern that looked like Figure 3.9.

Dr. Terry could have left it at that and allowed her system to remain an oscillating system. Fritz (1999) would call this situation "tolerable conflict." The conflict is still there. Conflicting structures are still clashing. Forward movement is still being counterbalanced by the philosophical positions and contradictory practices of the more traditional teams. Do you think that in the long run the overarching principles of student-centered learning, high expectations, integrated technology, and standards-based instruction would be equitably implemented for all students within the system if no further structural efforts were made? We'll return to a discussion of Bright Lake later in this chapter.

Structural Conflict and Tension-Resolution Systems at Country Elementary

Now, let's look at Country Elementary School's structural dynamics relative to their relationships with their parents. They were faced with a situation in which many of their students were

Figure 3.9   Another Tension-Resolution Pattern at Bright
Lake—Tolerable Conflict?

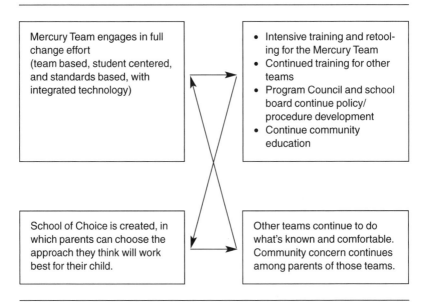

not achieving well, their attendance was poor, and the school was receiving a large number of parent complaints. That led them to contact the parents and call for more parent conferences in hopes of cajoling parents into getting more involved in their child's education and becoming more dedicated to sending their children to school every day. Figure 3.10 shows what the first tension-resolution system looked like.

Without thinking through all of the structures in play, being simply in reactive mode, one might think that this strategy should work. However, this first tension-resolution strategy did not take into consideration the previous history of these parents. They had not had good experiences with school in the past; they had failed in school themselves—and now their children were failing, too. They were coming in to school to be told their children were failing and to "work" with their children in ways they did not understand, and they were being chided for not sending their children to school every day. In essence, they were being told that they were now failing as parents.

So, the structural conflict looked as it does in Figure 3.11. You can see how some teachers might make momentary inroads with

Figure 3.10 Country Day Elementary, Parent Complaint Tension-Resolution System

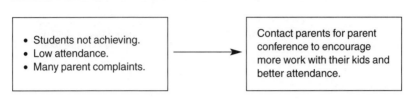

Figure 3.11 Structural Conflict—Parent Involvement at Country Day Elementary

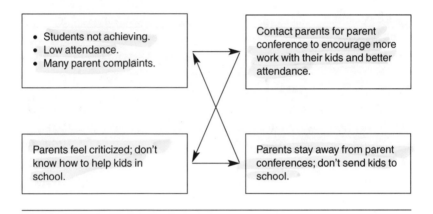

some parents, but, overall, this basic oscillating pattern stayed the same until the principal made some very basic structural changes.

Structural Conflict and Tension-Resolution Systems at City High

Let's look at the structural dynamics at City High School relative to their service delivery for students who need additional learning support. The principal and staff had become aware that there were many students in need of additional learning support in order to be successful in their general education classes. This led them to create resource rooms where students would receive the needed additional support. Students

Figure 3.12 Student Support Tension-Resolution System at City High

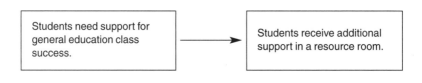

would leave the general education classroom and go to the resource room to receive assistance in the area in which they were struggling. Figure 3.12 shows what the first tension-resolution system looked like.

However, what actually occurred was that the support provided in the resource room was not connected to the general education curriculum. The resource teachers provided additional support, but the curriculum and expectations in the resource room were different from the general education classroom. This led to lower expectations for these students and increased the students' dependency on the resource teachers and their support. This certainly did not lead to the increased academic success in the general education classroom the staff had initially intended. In addition, this did not increase the students' use of effective instructional strategies or assist them in becoming responsible for their own learning. So, the structural conflict looks like Figure 3.13.

These examples push us to ask how one knows what changes to make. Can you change a structural conflict? No. You can't actually make this situation any different than it is. This structure is the way it is. What you can do is thoroughly analyze the structures and come to understand all of the forces at play, as these principals did. Principal Joy in the Country Elementary School came to understand that the parents were not comfortable coming to school for parent conferences. Dr. Terry came to understand that it would not work to link the forward movement of the Mercury Team to movement of the other teams. The City High administrators and staff came to understand that the resource room was not effective in increasing the student's success in the general education curriculum. But what then? If you can't fix the structures or the conflicts, what can you do? You can get clear about your values and priorities and create new advancing structures, which are free of conflicts.

Figure 3.13   Student Support System—Structural Conflict at City High

Students need support for general education class success.	Students receive additional support in a resource room.
Resource room support is not connected to the curriculum and expectations in the general education classroom.	Students are held to lower expectations, develop increased dependency on their resource room teachers, and are not successful in general education.

CREATING AN ADVANCING STRUCTURE THROUGH CLEAR VALUES

We have to decide what we really want to create, rather than try to react to and try to fix the old structures. Fritz (1999) tells us that "structural conflicts are not problems to be solved but structures that need to be redesigned" (p. 135). We have to redesign our structures so that we can move from a structure of conflict to a structure of advancement.

Let's go back to the Country Elementary School example and see how Principal Joy designed a new structure. First, she began by asking where parents wanted to have meetings, and she discovered it was anywhere but at the school! And so she held parent conferences at the Wal-Mart store. Then, she was able to build an advancing structure in which she was truly able to capture parents' attention and begin to build trust so that teachers could help them understand the ways they could help their children at home with their lessons. She was then slowly able to begin to lure the parents into the school, and even there she built new structures. She began with entertaining parents with skits poking fun at the old ways they did things in the school, again in an effort to build parents' *parent education and involvement very important*

trust and to recognize that they understood the parents' concerns. So, over time, Principal Joy was able to build new structures that invited parents to become so involved that they not only participated fully in their child's educational program but even began to volunteer and become involved in the larger school program in support of the wider community of children.

Looking again at Bright Lake School, Dr. Terry designed a new structure for parent choice, which on the one hand allowed oscillation to continue but on the other hand allowed the Mercury Team to decouple and continue on its advancing course. In this way, she built a new structure. If she had let the work stop there, however, that would not have been enough. The larger system would have eventually deepened its oscillations and subsumed the Mercury Team, blocking its advancement.

Here's where we get to the important part: Dr. Terry, the Program Council, and the school board never lost sight of their most important values—their primary goal. They kept structural tension around creating a school (not just one team) that embodied the principles of team-based, student-centered, standards-based learning and technology integration. Dr. Terry and her leadership team recognized that they could not do everything at once and that some goals were subordinated to the primary goal. They kept their eye on the ball and kept the development work going forward with the Mercury Team. They continued training and development of the other teams but didn't force the issue or push them beyond their capacity. They continued community education in a myriad of ways. They developed an action planning process whereby every team was expected to set specific goals and design action plans in accordance with the target improvement goals of the school and the key principles of the vision.

At the same time, Dr. Terry allowed teams to move at different rates of speed, intensifying their training as they showed greater readiness, as they built their capacity. She also did the hard supervision work with those who were truly sabotaging or failing to perform adequately. Over time, more and more teams began to embody the practices and principles of the vision, and more parents expressed comfort and confidence in the new methods, choosing to have their children placed on those teams who were enacting the principles and practices aligned with the primary vision of the school. The advancing structure enabled the teams to build momentum, building success upon success.

At City High, Principal John asked the department chair in special education to form a Building Support Services Committee to examine how to deploy resource room teachers in new ways to support the teaching of the state standards to all students. The committee decided to assign special educators to academic departments and to support a co-teaching model across all subjects. Teacher teams were also given time to collaborate to increase the quality of their communication and co-planning. These new advancing structures ensured all teachers were teaching the general education curriculum to all students.

In all three schools—Country Elementary School, Bright Lake School, and City High—the principals developed *new* structures to enable them and their staffs to remain true to what mattered most to them, to what Fritz (1999) would refer to as a "hierarchy of values." If it had mattered more to have parent conferences in school (just like the old structure would have us do), the value of actually communicating with parents in service of their children's learning would have been secondary. If it had mattered more to keep every teacher happy and parents comfortable, the value of creating a learning environment that was more engaging for kids would have become secondary, at least for a while.

When the parent meetings were held in Wal-Mart, the negative associations with school for the parents were absent. Secondary choices were made in support of their primary choice. Teachers brought their work to the Wal-Mart store. It was more work for teachers, but it was a choice that resulted in achieving the primary result they were after: positive communication with parents. In Bright Lake a secondary choice was made to release the other teams from being forced to follow Mercury's lead in the second year of the change effort in service of the primary choice to allow the Mercury Team to continue to develop their model unmolested for a couple of years. At City High, co-teaching ensured that a common curriculum was being taught to all students.

In all three schools, they chose to create an advancing structure in pursuit of what mattered most. They created a hierarchy of values and pursued their aspirations relentlessly. They moved from structural conflict to structural tension (as described in Chapter 2) as they defined and pursued their primary goals. And in doing so, they reorganized the relationship between the competing goals in the conflicting systems. When they changed the structures, the relationship of competition was removed, and they were able to make continuous progress toward what mattered most to them.

LEADERSHIP HAS TO MAKE CLEAR CHOICES

In the previous discussion, we referred to primary and secondary choices. This distinction is critical when thinking through one's values. Schools are cluttered settings, where structural conflict is rampant. Whenever we embark upon any improvement effort, having a clear hierarchy of values will be of paramount importance, because there will inevitably be conflicts. Decisions need to be made about which choices are of primary importance and which are secondary. As we saw in the examples above, the teachers' lugging their materials to Wal-Mart was secondary to making parent conferences successful. The "typical" structure of all teams looking the same was secondary to giving the prototype Mercury Team breathing room to develop their model sufficiently to stand on its own.

Everyone wants their school to create the best possible student learning. But what learning is most important? We can't do it all. Which programs come first? Which improvement goals will be worked on first? All schools have improvement goals, but too many schools set their goals haphazardly—and often do so from a problem-solving perspective. They don't think through their primary and secondary choices. They create conflicting goals or outstrip the capacity of their system to deliver on those goals. They overwhelm their teachers with too many initiatives at once, because they are trying to "fix" everything at once. The worst time to expect people to adopt substantially new methods is when they feel overwhelmed. Ask teachers today how it's going, and notice how many will tell you they feel overwhelmed. This is the inevitable result within a problem-solving orientation.

Hard choices need to be made by school leaders. To create advancing structures, leaders must make a choice about what is most important. If no choice is made, no choice will be adequately satisfied or supported. Too many schools simply avoid choosing by pretending to choose everything. They are organized around keeping the peace, solving the problems, and balancing the competing forces arising from the layers and pockets of structural conflict.

Such situational modes of leadership are oriented toward maintaining a steady state, maintaining equilibrium—to not rocking the boat. This is a good way to support an oscillating structure. Refusing to make choices will not support creating what you want. It will not help you realize your goals and aspirations, because the competing efforts will neutralize each other, cancel each other out. That's what oscillating structures are designed to do! The path of least resistance is to oscillate between and among competing tension-resolution systems, never achieving or holding on to any of the goals for long.

Balancing acts create leadership vacuums that encourage educators to move into camps representing various elements of structural conflicts. Collaboration and learning come to a standstill, while people become embroiled in bemoaning the other camp's inability to understand the real situation. They think, "They just don't get it. If they'd only adopt *our* approach, everything would be fine!" Or we hear, "If they'd only leave us alone and let us do our jobs, everything would be fine!"

Schools without clear purposes and shared organizing principles (primary goals) are directionless, and everybody suffers. People are left to do the only thing they can do in a leadership vacuum: They compete. They don't have any choice but to self-organize into competing subsystems. They create their own direction and see the other camps as being unreasonable and uncooperative. Why? Because they have no unifying principle.

With a unifying principle (shared values and aspirations), schools can transcend their structural conflicts and move to a productive structural tension. They can transform the pendulum swing into an archer's bow. They can transform the frustration of "here we go again" to the joy of seeing a program on target. Everyone involved can see and understand their shared reality, and they can agree on actions and strategies that will move them toward their goals. When they sort out their hierarchical values and agree on what matters most, they can create an advancing path—one that leads to success, with increasing traction and momentum.

SUMMARY

In summary, let us leave you with a few guiding principles we hope you will remember as you move through your day-to-day work in your schools:

- Recognize that schools are burdened with too many goals. You can never do it all.
- Expect conflicting priorities whenever you are setting goals.
- Conflicting goals or too many goals will produce only temporary success or no success at all.
- Don't try to fix old structures; create new ones.
- Be clear about what goals are primary and what goals are secondary.
- Don't try to solve all the problems. Instead, focus on creating what really matters to you and the kids in the school.
- Leaders need to make clear choices and create a hierarchy of values that guide decision making throughout the system for everyone.

In the next chapter, we'll delve even more deeply into the purpose and principles of schools and explore how to create a solid foundation for your advancing structures to rest upon.

CHAPTER FOUR

Developing Shared Purposes and Principles

Elementary School Principal:	The purpose of our school is to educate kids so they are prepared for the future.
Middle School Principal:	The purpose of our school is to develop skills and help kids learn about themselves.
High School Principal:	The purpose of our school is to teach content so it can be applied in situations when they are out of school.
Elementary Teacher:	The purpose of our school is to help students learn so they can get through school and life.
Director of Special Education:	The purpose of schools in our district is to help students develop into productive community members and citizens.
Superintendent:	The purpose of schools in our district is to assist students in finding knowledge and to assist students in preparing for life beyond K–12 school.
Parent:	The purpose of our school is to give students the tools to be productive members of society.

S o, what is the purpose of our schools? We spend a lot of time talking about how to teach and how to organize our schools—and that's certainly important—but how do we think and talk about the purpose and principles of our schools? Why is our school important? Postman (1996) tells us schools need a "transcendent and honorable purpose in order to become the central institution through which the young may find reasons for continuing to educate themselves" (p. xi). Purpose provides a reason for students to learn and guides teachers and administrators in their collective work and decision making. This chapter will explore just what purpose is and why it's important. It will also highlight how our colleagues in Country Elementary and Bright Lake schools developed and identified their shared purposes and principles and will discuss how you might apply this work to your own school setting.

HOW DO WE DEFINE PURPOSE AND PRINCIPLES?

We begin with some definitions of purpose and principles because these concepts have been described and used in many different ways, which can easily lead to confusion as well as wasted time and energy. What do we mean by *purpose?* The purpose of an organization, including schools, is the "reason for being." An effective purpose reflects people's idealistic motivations for doing the work and is the organization's foundation (Collins & Porras, 1996; Fritz, 1996). Knowing the purpose of our schools helps us answer the question about why our schools exist.

Purpose and goals are different. Whereas goals are things we hope to achieve when we set them, purpose is different in that it is an ongoing force that is continually in play within the organization. An organization's purpose becomes clear to the organization's members when they work with others in the organization: when they see what others believe the organization stands for, what aspirations they have for the organization, what excites and disappoints them, what their hope for the organization is, what pride they have in their past accomplishments, and what their desire for the future is (Fritz, 1996). Although the purpose itself does not change, it should inspire change, because it is something that is sought after and desired.

How is that different from *principles?* The principles of a school are its core values. Core values are the essential and enduring tenets of an organization or school that support and are in pursuit of the purpose (Collins & Porras, 1996). The school's core values stand the test of time and don't change in response to external factors. Core values are fundamental and so deeply held that they will seldom, if ever, change.

Why Are Purpose and Principles So Important in a School?

Imagine yourself working in a school whose purpose is unclear. How do you as a teacher design the work if you don't know the reason for the work? Without clear purpose, how can you as a teacher make teaching and learning interesting and engaging for students? Why do students think they are in school if the teachers don't know the overall purpose? How do teachers and administrators make decisions about their work if they don't know why they are doing what they are doing? How do teachers and administrators know how to work with each other if they don't know where they are headed? How do schools engage their community without knowing their purpose? Purpose and principles guide us in making sense of why we are doing our work as well as how we should do our work.

Unless educators have inspiring and transcending purposes for schools, children will see schools as pointless and have limited reason to learn (Postman, 1996). Educators with a strong sense of purpose and principles create a public that is confident, that has a shared sense of purpose and a respect for learning and diversity.

When schools know their purpose, they can make decisions that are consistent with their desired direction and purpose. This can apply to a whole host of decisions, including decisions about curriculum, policies, and procedures; about what knowledge and skills need to be developed; about resources and about activities for the future. A common purpose will keep the work focused and moving forward. All too often, isolated purposes and sometimes conflicting purposes take the work in unintended and nonproductive directions. When the purpose is clear, daily decisions are guided and measured against that purpose, thereby creating more potential for advancement of the desired results.

Coming to know the school's principles helps the staff define what they and their school stand for, what they want to achieve, and what prevents them from allowing their own reactions and responses solely to guide their work. It is important to recognize that organizations actually choose their true principles by the actions they take, the decisions they make, and the plans and strategies to which they commit (Fritz, 1996). Fritz explains that our choices actually define for us what we truly value most and that our attitudes are defined by our actions rather than by our claims. An organization with clear principles can be counted on to behave consistently, and thus to make sense to the people in it and the people served by it. Such an organization has the potential to remain focused and disciplined in pursuit of its purpose. Just as with purpose, principles help guide all kinds of decisions about things ranging from curriculum to budget to hiring practices while unifying the people and their work.

How Do We Identify Our Purpose and Principles?

We have all worked in some type of district or school improvement team in which we were required to describe our school's purpose, principles, mission, and so forth. This experience probably involved working in teams and producing rich and inspiring insights. Then, we were required to reduce these complex ideas into simple statements that could be posted around the school. Or these statements were turned into a muddled conglomeration of values, goals, purposes, and practices expressed in generic language while the deep and valuable insights were lost due to the need to compromise to meet all of the team members' wordsmithing wishes. Unfortunately, the value and the meaning of the thinking are frequently lost by the time the final draft has been completed.

We suggest a different way to think about developing shared purpose and principles. First of all, this should not be an exercise in wordsmithing and should not take hours and hours. The point is not to create a perfect statement but to gain a deep understanding of the school's purpose and principles, which can be expressed in a multitude of ways (Collins & Porras, 1996). One powerful way for getting at purpose is the *five whys* (Collins & Porras, 1996). Start with a descriptive statement of purpose and then ask, "Why is that important?" . . . five times. After a few whys, you will most likely find that you're getting deeper into the school's fundamental purpose.

Fritz (1996) suggests, however, that purpose may be difficult for members of an organization to articulate even though it can often be felt and recognized. While Fritz recognizes the importance of purpose as a unifying theme in an organization, he doesn't talk about it very much with his clients. Rather, he sees how it comes up when they talk about the organization's work, when they describe what excites and disappoints them, what they hope for, and what they value.

When it comes to identifying the principles, we don't believe it can be done by merely making a list and getting consensus. Fritz (1996) reminds us that an organization chooses its true values by the actions it takes and the decisions it makes. As stated earlier, our choices define what we value most. Therefore, we need to look closely at our organizational actions and decisions and ask ourselves with brutal honesty whether our choices truly reflect the values and principles we say we believe in. If we find a conflict between our values and our actions, we either need to change our values or our choices.

We suggest a process for identifying principles by incorporating observation, feedback, and dialogue on your organizational decisions and choices. We can simply observe what matters most to people and find emerging patterns or themes. This information can be shared with the staff through a dialogue to show them what seems to be valued as well as to increase awareness about some principles the staff may not have explored explicitly. Given the areas that seem to take priority, staff can then make decisions about which principles are most dominant in their work. Clearly, the intent is for all individuals to understand what is guiding their work and develop some shared ownership and acceptance regarding this common focus.

Now that we have an idea of what we mean by *purpose* and *principles* and how to think about developing shared purpose and principles, let's look at how our colleagues in Country Elementary School and Bright Lake School tackled these issues. These two schools developed their purpose and principles in very different ways, and we ask you to consider what aspects will work best for you in your context as you read their stories.

COUNTRY ELEMENTARY SCHOOL

Country Elementary School took a long time to develop shared purposes and principles—six years! As you might recall from their story, Country Elementary never really took the time collectively to think about their purpose and principles and was not motivated for any reason to think about them. Staff at the school just went along from day to day, worked hard, and didn't question why they did what they did or what they could do differently. Their student achievement scores were at or slightly below the state average, and the teachers, students, and community just came to accept this status and level of functioning as their way. There was limited urge for anything new to be done in the schools—that is, until the community began to change and families were moving in from trailer park neighborhoods that were redistricted within this school community.

The school felt the impact of the changing community quickly as classes increased in size. Teachers didn't know their students or families anymore, they didn't know how to teach students with different learning needs, and discipline issues increased in and out of the school. The teachers found they were working harder and harder and getting more and more frustrated because they were not feeling successful with the students. After a few years of observing staff frustration escalate, the principal finally recognized something needed to be done. She wasn't sure what, but she knew this was no longer acceptable.

Principal Joy began by having staff meetings and listening intently to the teachers' frustrations and issues. She met with staff individually to hear their stories. She observed classes and got to know the students and their families. What she learned over this time is that staff cared a great deal about the students: They were committed to the students, they were willing to work hard with long hours, but they didn't know what to do, they didn't have anything that tied them together or provide a purpose to their teaching. They were confused and stuck in their ways, just getting through each day as best as they could and becoming more and more exhausted. They were in an oscillating structure that had no clear purpose or direction. The staff's learning was not coordinated with any purpose, their daily decisions were not guided by known principles, they had limited time to talk to each other, and the community was rapidly growing and changing. These conditions lead to structural oscillation and caused a significant amount of frustration among the staff.

The purpose and principles for Country Elementary School were articulated after six years in which the principal, staff, and community worked together to figure out what they wanted for this school and how it was going to improve. This was accomplished through various types of informal and formal meetings with staff, students, and community members. They all eventually came to agree that the purpose of the school was to engage all students in learning opportunities that would prepare them to make choices about their futures. They had ongoing dialogue about what this future looked like and how it would come into being. There were many choices they needed to make about how they would achieve these improvements; however, once the staff came to understand their old ways of working were no longer consistent with their desired future, they were able to commit to doing things differently. They had achieved some clarity about what they wanted to do and why they wanted to do it and had some beginning dialogue about how they would begin this process.

The principles that support their overall school purpose were also articulated and aligned throughout this six-year process. While the principal was facilitating the discussions about their future and what they all wanted to see for the students and families, she kept note of what mattered most to them and what their choices represented. She would frequently feed her observations back to the staff and ask for validation and clarification. This occurred several times, and each time some type of modification was made in the principles. The staff at Country Elementary eventually created what they call their "10 givens," which represent for them their guiding principles. Figure 4.1 highlights some of these principles.

It should be clear that the development of shared purposes and principles in Country Elementary School was an emergent process that took several years. After approximately 10 years, the purposes and principles are very clear to the staff and community, based on how the teachers and parents work together and the nature of the teaching and learning in the school. They revisit the

Figure 4.1   Country Elementary's 10 Givens

- Provide high-quality and engaging work to all students.
- Accept responsibility for all students.
- Keep all students in school and in class.
- Provide a safe and caring environment.
- Be prepared and ready to teach each day.
- Work in a collegial and collaborative manner.
- Engage in schoolwide professional development.
- Create quality learning for all students.
- Respect all parents and community members.
- Expect parents to get their children to school every day and see that homework is completed.

principles and purposes frequently so as to keep them alive and guiding their work.

We have several questions for you about this particular story. Do you think it should take so much time? Is there any way to speed up the process while not compromising on creating meaning and understanding? What happens when you try to make it happen more quickly? We know each context has its own set of issues and there are no easy answers; however, the next story may help illuminate some ways to answer these questions.

BRIGHT LAKE SCHOOL

As you recall from the initial story, when Dr. Terry began at Bright Lake School, the school board already had a fairly clear idea about what was important to them. The school board, along with a small group of teachers from Bright Lake, had developed together their purpose and principles for the school. They collectively determined that the purpose of their school was to prepare students for post-school success while engaging all students in the process. They supported ideas and principles related to student centeredness with

Figure 4.2   Bright Lake's Guiding Principles

- All students can learn everything we feel it is important for them to know.

- The educational program is focused on constructing meaning and discovering knowledge.

- Standards and research-based instruction practices drive curriculum and instruction.

- We can create schools where learning is a constant and time a variable.

- Families of learners involve parents, students, and other significant adults in determining learning goals leading to personal plans for every student.

- Technology will enhance learning opportunities for all students.

- Innovation is an ongoing process.

- Authentic assessment and real world demonstrations are integrated into all projects.

an enriched curriculum that integrated technology into the instruction. When Dr. Terry began her position as principal, this work had just been completed. Figure 4.2 highlights their guiding principles.

At this time, one team in the school embraced these ideas while most of the others remained satisfied with their current teaching and learning. This one team worked with the school board in the development of the purpose and principles. Dr. Terry decided to use the first year to examine the purpose and principles underlying student-centered learning. She did this by meeting with staff and community members and discussing their questions, concerns, and ideas. Within the first year and through a significant amount of deliberation, they did create an overall understanding of their purpose and what was guiding their work. The ideas needed to become clear and concrete so as to facilitate their real meaning.

During the second year, there was a heavy focus on building the staff's capacity to implement student-centered learning. The principal utilized such supports as mentors, release time, and summer institutes and allocated resources as needed. By the end of the second year, 7 of the 10 school teams embraced the principles. Dr. Terry kept the direction clear, advanced the work, and continued to build capacity among the teams over the next several years. By the end of the sixth year, 8 of the 10 school teams embraced the principles, while two teams were only giving minimal attention to the learner-centered principles.

CITY HIGH SCHOOL

The superintendent of the school district and Principal John came to understand the purpose of City High School when their concerns about student achievement were validated with test score results. The results indicated that although 77% of the students were passing the high-stakes state test, minority students and students with exceptional learning needs were significantly below state expectations. The superintendent and Principal John were also beginning to deal with the No Child Left Behind Act and were clear that something needed to change. They together decided the purpose of City High School was to assure all students achieved at high levels.

With data as support, the principal discussed the issues as well as the purpose of City High School with his leadership cabinet, which included assistant principals and directors of programs. He also discussed the same issues with department chairs as well as teachers during small-group discussions held during the school day. The data were so powerful that there was no disagreement that something needed to change. The purpose of the school became clear and this work became an immediate priority.

To begin to work on resolving these issues, Principal John asked the department chairs to recommend teachers to serve on a Planning Committee, which would be charged with using data and any other resources to assist them in understanding why achievement was so low for some student groups and what could be done to change this pattern. Planning Committee participants were given time during the day to do this work and were also scheduled a common lunch time if the committee wanted to work during this time as well. Principal John offered this committee inservice

[margin note: Visit other schools]

opportunities about diversity as well and offered site visits to other schools who were demonstrating success with all students. Committee participants attended a national conference on increasing minority performance and observed schools in a neighboring state that were successful with minority students. Principal John visited the Planning Committee periodically to show his interest, commitment, and support. He continued to highlight the purpose and importance of their work.

[margin note: principal attended mtgs]

The Planning Committee made several recommendations to the high school faculty that would support the principle that all students should achieve at high levels. They recommended that all student groups be enrolled in more advanced preparation (AP) courses and indicated that the AP courses needed to be redesigned with the Planning Committee's input, that more teachers were needed to deliver the AP courses, and that students and teachers needed to stay together for a two-year period. It took one year to put these recommendations in place, and within two years more minority students were enrolled in AP courses and had higher grade point averages than their peers who were not enrolled in these courses.

[margin note: student only offered high level classes]

City High differs from our other stories in that Principal John and the staff did not explicitly discuss their guiding principles. Rather, the principles emerged during their work together and are embedded in the daily practice and conversations of not only Principal John but also numerous administrators and teachers. In addition, the principles are clearly reflected in the professional development provided for the school staff. Figure 4.3 outlines the principles that guide their work.

Principal John identified the achievement gap in City High School as immoral. The school's efforts and early success have been recognized by many in the state for its work in decreasing this achievement gap.

LESSONS LEARNED FROM OUR STORIES

Although the contexts were different, all three principals at our sample schools maintained the direction and advanced the system as opposed to getting caught up and carried away by the system oscillations. The principals also focused on the *meaning* of the

Figure 4.3   City High's Guiding Principles

- Establish a culture of responsibility to have all students learn at high levels.
- All students have access to all opportunities and resources to ensure equity of access and equity of outcome.
- Understand that high expectations lead to higher levels of achievement.
- Understand that higher levels of achievement require higher levels of support.
- Increase peer support for higher expectations to increase student motivation.
- Professional development is continuous.
- Empower staff with data and provide time to learn together.

Had Staff book of data and make decisions.

purpose and principles, not just getting something written to say it's done. Although there was significant dialogue and deliberation throughout their work and although all voices were pursued, not everyone was involved in developing the purpose and principles. Everyone had multiple opportunities to contribute; however, the principals needed to make it all come together. The principals reflected on what mattered; they matched choices, decisions, and actions to values and principles. They engaged in dialogue to clarify people's thinking and to align values to the actions. They illuminated structural conflict and made hierarchical choices. They all understood it was absolutely necessary to maintain certain dominant themes and goals.

Fritz (1996) helps us end the myth that everyone needs to be an author of the work in order for it to be shared. He reminds us that if a vision is truly shared, we participate in it because we care about it and will support it. It is not just because we authored something that we share it. Fritz goes so far as to say that "if the vision matters more to us because we had a hand in creating it, then the vision's intrinsic value must be in question or we have our focus in the wrong place" (p. 199). Especially in Bright Lake School, the purpose and principles were well created by the board and small team of teachers, and it was then up to Dr. Terry and her staff to enact the values and principles in their day-to-day choices, decisions, and actions.

The need to prioritize was also critical in all three cases. The principals seemed to carve their work out from year to year so as not to overwhelm themselves or their staff. They determined what mattered most and also prioritized certain values over others. Once they knew their predominant values, they then determined their primary goals. These primary goals were the focal point in organizing structural tension. Once they knew the primary goals, the other competing outcomes were organized to support the goal. This helped keep their work moving forward as opposed to getting off track and sucked into oscillation and structural conflict.

All schools had a significant amount of stress and turmoil and the main issues could have easily gotten lost. Principal Joy of Country Elementary School continued to emphasize how important it was to "keep the main thing, the main thing!" She and her staff created an advancing pattern in which they paid attention to what they were trying to create and then organized their resources around making it happen. Principal John of City High was extremely focused on making sure all students achieved to high levels and was guided by this every single day.

All three principals continually revisited their purpose and principles with their staff and community for several reasons. They wanted not only to keep the focus clear, but also to keep moving staff and the community in the direction of the purpose. They recognized this wasn't a one-shot deal and that having a clear understanding of the purpose and principles was critical to guiding the school's work. They recognized the importance of building momentum, of organizing things so that each success created a foundation and impetus for the next success.

Time is certainly an issue. What is the right amount of time to develop shared purpose and principles? Country Elementary School took up to six years while Bright Lake School tried to accomplish this part of their work in two years. It certainly depends on your context; however, we are all probably in agreement that we just can't wait 10 years if we are certain that the conditions for teaching and learning are not supportive for all students. Dr. Terry from Bright Lake School has reflected that perhaps they tried to accomplish their work too quickly and needed more time to establish a shared understanding of their purpose and principles. On the other hand, the principal of

Country Elementary School recognizes that six years is a long time but believes they actually needed that time to figure out what was going on and then develop some type of plan. Principal John at City High knew they couldn't wait another day to get focused and started on this work and is fairly satisfied with the results they achieved within a three-year time frame.

SUMMARY

In summary, developing shared purpose and principles is critical in our work. Without it, we don't know where we are going, why we are going there, and how to work on a day-to-day basis. Our choices and decisions inevitably lead us into structural conflict, because the hard choices are not being made in alignment with values and principles aligned with what matters most. While there is a great deal you will need to decide based on your local issues, following are some guiding tips:

- Establish a hierarchy of values that will guide hard decisions in the direction of what matters most.
- Involve all voices and pursue those that don't immediately stand out, but at the same time understand that one need not be an author in order to be a supporter of purpose and principles.
- Use language that is as clear and concrete as possible to maximize its understanding, and recognize that it is not possible to ever fully capture the depth of meaning really wrapped up in the heartfelt purposes and deepest values in our work.
- Listen intently to what people are saying is important to them, because this is how the understanding of purposes and principles is continually refreshed and clarified.
- Establish an environment in which it is safe for people to have an honest dialogue about their views.
- Stay focused on the nature and direction of the work.
- Use the tension between what you want and where you are productively.
- Give it time . . . but not too much!

CHAPTER FIVE

Building Democratic Community in a Diverse Society

M any of us are familiar with schools where teachers work in isolation, where teachers have minimal time in their schedules to talk with each other about student learning and other important educational issues, where teachers have minimal opportunity to voice critical questions or raise issues regarding their work, and where parents and the surrounding community are thought of and treated as separate entities from the life of the school.

Given this fairly common scenario, we shouldn't be surprised when teachers and parents are skeptical when school leaders talk about building a community of learners in which teachers and parents can share their ideas and expertise and have a voice in the various issues and demands made of schools. How can we expect teachers to build and engage in a community of learners when the conditions and structures are in such contradiction to this very notion? How can we expect parents to believe us and feel welcome in the school when we minimize their roles and participation? Many individuals may be well-intentioned, may even desperately desire to engage in a new practice and build a community, but are absolutely not able to given the conditions and structures in which they work.

This chapter will explore what we mean by *community*, discuss how to build a community, review some of the research that supports its priority in the schools, and revisit our colleagues to learn how they worked on community building in their schools.

WHAT DO WE MEAN BY *DEMOCRATIC COMMUNITY*?

The concept of community is rather complex and is used in multiple ways in the education literature. Furman and Starratt (2002) suggest we can no longer think of community as a place in which a sense of belonging is achieved through identification with people who are "like us." These types of communities, such as places of worship, will always be important in our lives, but it is no longer a realistic notion for schools characterized by diversity of race, class, ability, ethnicity, sexual orientation, and language. In addition, schools can no longer effectively function in isolation from the broader community given the complexity of social and economic issues facing our students and families.

Furman and Starratt (2002) encourage us to think about a democratic community that emphasizes the idea of a "community of difference," in which "difference is celebrated but interdependence is recognized, and the common good, locally and globally, is the glue" (p. 116). A democratic community recognizes the interdependence of the school and the surrounding community and includes parents as well as the broader community into the system.

Following are some common themes that emerge regarding the nature or character of democratic community:

- Democratic community is based on open inquiry with full and free interplay of ideas.
- Democratic community members work for the common good.
- In democratic community, the rights of all, including the less powerful, are respected.

Figure 5.1 An Adapted Framework for a Democratic Community

very # Important

Potential Benefits of a Democratic Community

- Empowerment of faculty, students, parents, and community members
- Collective responsibility for student's learning by all stakeholders
- Improvement in student learning

Characteristics of a Democratic Community

- Ethic of difference
- Shared values
- Reflective dialogue
- Deprivatization of practice
- Focus on student learning
- Collaboration

Structural Conditions That Support a Democratic Community

- Time to meet and talk
- Physical proximity
- Interdependent teaching, parent, and community roles[a]
- Communication structures
- Teacher/parent empowerment and school autonomy
- Accurate and timely accountability data
- A school improvement framework

Social and Human Resources That Support a Democratic Community

- Openness to improvement
- Trust and respect
- Cognitive skill development
- Accessing expertise, ideas, and resources
- Supportive leadership
- Socialization

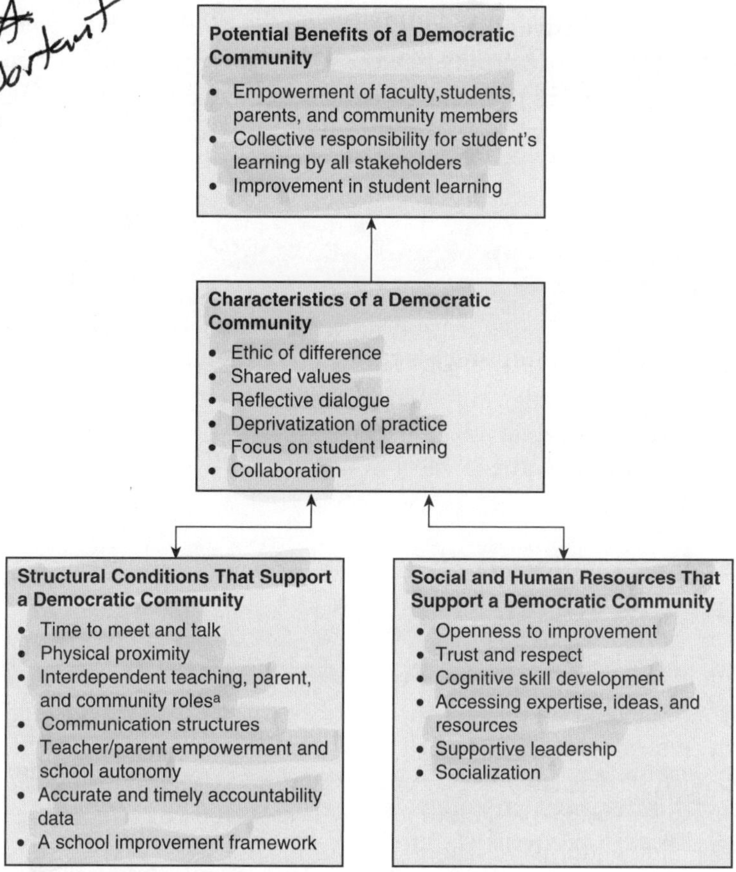

NOTE: [a] Roles are not separate and distinct in a democratic community.

- Creating democratic community in schools is a systemic challenge, involving structures, processes, and curriculum. (Furman & Starratt, 2002)

We have taken the elements derived from the research of Louis and Kruse (1995) on *professional community* and extended the concept of professional community to include all stakeholders in a school-based democratic community. Figure 5.1 represents the critical elements for developing a democratic community.

A democratic community shows itself in schools in multiple ways. We would see teachers working with each other, learning from each other, and questioning each other about their practices. We would see the principal listening to the voices of the teachers, parents, and students to deeply understand their perspectives and issues. We would see parents and community members initiating participation in school activities and forums and being welcomed and accepted within this role. We would see parents, teachers, and principals working together toward a common goal. We would see teachers working with students in respectful ways, encouraging their voice and input, and implementing a curriculum that teaches students to ask questions and be skeptical about certain things when confronted with various viewpoints or knowledge. Essentially, we would see students, parents, community members, and teachers having voice, being involved in the school, and not excluding one group or class at the expense of others.

HOW DO WE BUILD A DEMOCRATIC COMMUNITY?

Building a democratic community is both a process and a moral activity. Let's first consider the processes of democratic participation that are needed to create this community. First, we need to establish structures and procedures that allow all members of the community to participate and have a respected voice in decisions and policies that affect them (Furman & Starratt, 2002; Louis & Kruse, 1995). We also need to create structures that are intimate enough so teachers, parents, and students can think, talk, and make decisions together. There needs to be the time to socialize, meet, and talk, as well as communication structures to promote and continue the dialogue. We need to create opportunities for staff to develop the necessary knowledge, skills, and dispositions to respond to new practices in curriculum, instruction, and assessment. We need to create conditions in which teachers make their practices more public, collaborate with their peers and parents, and talk with each other about student learning and school issues. This dialogue should take place not only in formal committee structures or councils but also through informal and spontaneous interactions.

Democratic participation, however, requires more than creating forums and councils: It also requires an openness to improvement and an ability to listen, understand, empathize, respect, trust, negotiate, debate, and resolve conflicts in a spirit that recognizes their common good and interdependence (Furman & Starratt, 2002; Louis & Kruse, 1995). Moreover, we need to focus on the means for reaching the goals and learn how to create an environment in which everyone has the chance to openly express his or her thoughts and feelings, in which these are received without argument or judgment, and in which this process is continued until larger understandings are achieved (Furman & Starratt, 2002).

Along with the type of structures, communication, and dialogue needed in democratic community, there is the social morality that guides the community to recognize the worth of individuals and the social value of community, to celebrate difference, and to understand the ultimate interdependence of all. In addition, there must be a commitment to civility and collective action. Furman and Starratt (2002) suggest this moral sense has several dimensions:

- There is a value in coming together in the interest of the common good.
- There is a value in open inquiry and critique in the pursuit of the common good.
- There is respect for individuals and celebration of differences.
- There is a responsibility that acknowledges the interdependence of all in achieving the common good.

In summary, schools that seek to create democratic community need to consider processes, structures, and values for this work. The following section will briefly describe why we believe democratic community is so important in our schools.

WHY IS DEMOCRATIC COMMUNITY SO IMPORTANT?

Although research focusing on the impact of democratic community on student learning is relatively new, there are some case studies that do show that relational trust among teachers, parents, students, and school leaders improves student learning and is a key resource for school improvement and reform (Bryk & Schneider, 2003). *Relational trust* here is defined as having respect, personal regard, and personal integrity—some of the dimensions required in democratic community. Bryk and Schneider (2003) found that elementary schools with high relational trust were much more likely to demonstrate marked improvements in student learning. This overall measure was determined to be a powerful discriminator between improving and nonimproving schools. Another significant finding of Bryk and Schneider was that schools with chronically weak trust had virtually no chance of improving in either reading or mathematics.

Similarly, the School Development Project demonstrated that strengthening the connections between urban school professionals and parents of low socioeconomic status and creating a community of respect and collaboration can improve their children's academic achievement (Comer, Haynes, Joyner, & Ben-Avie, 1996). And in a study that compared public and private schools, Bryk, Lee, and Holland (1993) found that a sense of community was a key factor in cultivating a sense of excellence in private schools. Teachers in these more communal schools were more satisfied with their work, were seen by students as enjoying teaching, and were less likely to be absent. Students in these schools were less likely to misbehave, were less likely to drop out, and showed higher gains in mathematic achievement.

Finally, Meier (1995) argues that building trust among teachers, students, families, and school leaders was a key component in the success of the reform of a middle school in Harlem, New York, which yielded significantly improved student learning. The small school size created a more intimate learning environment and provided conditions that allowed teachers, students, families, and school leaders to have a voice in the teaching and learning process.

We believe democratic community is critical for student learning. Next to the family, the school has the most significant impact on children's growth and development. We need to commit to working with, listening to, and respecting each other. As we do this, we need to commit to providing and promoting the processes, structures, and values of a democratic community to make it happen.

Let's now return to the stories of our colleagues and see what they can teach us about democratic community.

COUNTRY ELEMENTARY SCHOOL

As you recall, Country Elementary School was characterized by extreme teacher frustration, low academic achievement, and minimal parental trust and involvement. The Country Elementary story actually shows the building of democratic community in many ways.

To begin, when the staff came to the realization that they needed to change their expectation for student learning, the principal encouraged staff to explore various models of school improvement. There was openness to improvement, openness to staff exploring, dialoguing, and ultimately coming to unanimous agreement on what direction they would take regarding curriculum, instruction, and assessment. They all understood this was a significant challenge that involved getting at the core aspects of authentic teaching and learning. With the principal's guidance and leadership, the staff came to understand their commitment to all children and the common good, which is a key aspect of a democratic community.

The Country Elementary staff also figured out how to work with each other as well as how to engage the parents in the school. As we recall, the principal created time for staff to meet and plan together. School meetings were redesigned to be less about business and procedural issues and more about dialogue about relevant issues. Parent meetings were redesigned when Principal Joy asked the parents, "Where and when can we talk to you?" When the parents answered "Wal-Mart," that is where Principal Joy and her staff had their meetings.

In time, the parents decided they could begin meeting with the staff in the school. The staff built trust by listening to the parents, having personal regard for their situations, and being authentic about their intentions. The principal also implemented forums with the staff and larger community to discuss important educational issues and learn the different participants' perspectives regarding schooling. This reflective dialogue continued to build trust as well as to create a collective focus on teaching and learning.

Now, Country Elementary School has parents running every noncurricular event, attending 100% of student conferences, and substituting in the classroom to support teacher collaboration and professional development time, and some parents have even pursued obtaining their teaching licenses because they now want to teach in a place like Country Elementary School. The democratic community in Country Elementary includes and respects everyone, even the less powerful, which is another key factor in a democratic community.

Principal Joy of Country Elementary School set the moral tone for the school as they began to change, and the school now represents all of the key moral dimensions of a democratic community. By listening to each other, parents and staff began to value the need to work together and focus on the common good for all children. They valued open inquiry and exploring all avenues of teaching and learning before they decided on their model. They began to respect all learners and all families and started to have high expectations for everyone. Finally, they came to understand their interdependence by admitting that they were all responsible for all children and that staff and parents could not accomplish what they wanted for all children without working together.

BRIGHT LAKE SCHOOL

As you recall, the Bright Lake School story begins with a team of teachers working with the school board to establish a set of guiding principles and vision for their school. In this example of democratic community building, this team was given the opportunity to engage in inquiry with each other and, with the support of the school board, to lead the school toward a new set of practices. They were concerned about all students, not just a segment of their student population, as they explored and established their principles, vision, and practices.

As you know, when the principal began at Bright Lake, she inherited this work from the school board and team of teachers, and she found it consistent with her own vision for the school. Dr. Terry quickly learned, however, that not all of the Bright Lake staff were supportive of this new vision and were unwilling to engage in all of the new practices. Being sensitive to democratic community, Dr. Terry supported each team as they explored these new ideas and helped them build their knowledge and skills in ways that were meaningful to them. She built structures that helped these teams to learn from each other, question each other, and ultimately implement the learner-centered principles within their mutually agreed-upon time frame. She created a management team (the Program Council) to share information and expertise with all teams and to begin to make their collective work more public to each other. All teachers had a voice in the process and were supported in coming to understand the power of the principles, vision, and practices.

While this was occurring, Dr. Terry learned that not all parents were supportive of these new ideas either. She again demonstrated an important element of democratic community by including parents in this dialogue and learning process. Parents had an equal voice in this schoolwide transformation process. An equivalent structure to the Program Council, called the Families as Partners Council, was created to support the conversation between parents and the Bright Lake staff. Parents were invited to participate in forums to share their concerns and questions, to observe classrooms, and to have access to information that would assist them in understanding the instructional framework. The principal built strong communication structures so that parents, teachers, and Dr. Terry were having an ongoing dialogue about the principles, vision, and practices. The parents recommended changes regarding such things as classroom organization, design of IEPs, and quiet space for learning. In response to the parent recommendations, the principal and teachers provided parents with weekly information demonstrating how their recommendations for change were being implemented in the classrooms. Dr. Terry modeled the value of coming together, having open inquiry and critique, and the interdependence of all in achieving the common good.

Democratic community was also represented in how the teams of teachers, students, and parents actually planned a student's program. IEPs were developed for all students in the school and were designed collaboratively by the teacher, student, and parent. Although all student plans were guided by the learning standards, all had a voice in how the instructional program would be implemented as well as how to personalize the plans so as to build on specific student interests, strengths, and needs.

In summary, Bright Lake School, like Country Elementary School, built trust with staff and parents through reflective dialogue, listening, having personal regard for the others' situations, and being authentic and honest about their intentions. The communication structures set in place for the staff and parents, the management team, and the personal student plans were all examples of structures Dr. Terry and her staff put in place to advance the system to the desired learner-centered instructional framework. Dr. Terry knew this work needed to be done with support, voice, and involvement from the teachers, parents, and surrounding community. A democratic community was created and was critical to the implementation of the principles, vision, and learner-centered practices throughout the school.

CITY HIGH SCHOOL

The City High story provides two dramatic examples of how the principal and staff confronted some damaging practices that were obstacles to creating a democratic community. This story is about how the principal makes these issues a priority and how the staff ultimately work for the common good, respect the rights of all students, and challenge the system to create new structures, processes, and curriculum.

A common practice in City High School was to exclude students with disabilities from participating in a choir performance in the community during the holiday season. When Principal John learned about this practice, he and his staff immediately created a new course policy of universal access for all students. The process for course assignments changed and all students were given the opportunity to experience all aspects of the school, including academic, extracurricular, and student support activities. Principal John recognized the high school was clearly not a democratic community unless all students were included in the life of the school, had a voice, and were respected for their differences. This one issue of the choir performance was the catalyst for creating new structures, processes, and curriculum so as to build democratic community in the high school.

Another dramatic example at City High is reflected in Principal John's response to the low academic achievement of African American male students. The principal talked directly to the students and staff about this disturbing trend. He challenged the students to take more responsibility for their learning and challenged the staff to confront their low expectations for these students. In order to get these students engaged in the school and their learning, Principal John created a new cohort structure of students and staff. The students were able to develop relationships with each other and learn in ways that engaged their interests, and they were encouraged to enroll in prerequisite courses for advanced placement courses. These students are now achieving at a higher rate while taking part in more of these prerequisite courses than the average City High School student.

Both of these examples demonstrate the moral tone set by the principal. He was committed to the moral aspects of democratic community and was working for the good of all students. He encouraged inquiry into the situation and promoted reflective dialogue with students and staff. The rights of all, including the less powerful, were respected. Principal John's response was to redesign structures, processes, and the curriculum so as to begin to build democratic community.

LESSONS LEARNED FROM OUR STORIES

The three principals in our stories genuinely cared about all of the students and families and knew they would not have a whole school unless all were involved and represented. Country Elementary and Bright Lake viewed parents and the surrounding community as a part of the school and invited them legitimately to participate in the transformation process. Parents were not passive receivers of information but were contributing team members who played key roles in all aspects of the school. The principals acknowledged the interdependence of all in achieving the common good for all students.

All of the principals also recognized there were both structural issues as well as social and moral issues involved in building democratic community. They recognized from the beginning that some structures were interfering with the teachers and parents even talking to each other. Time and communication structures were immediately created to enable the work to begin. The principals promoted inquiry, critique, and reflective dialogue among staff, students, and parents. They encouraged their staff to make their teaching practices public so all could learn from each other. They empowered their staff to make instructional decisions and use data to determine the effectiveness of their work. The principals did not lose sight of the overall vision even when there was controversy and differences of opinion. While they continually modified their activities based on input, they did not change the priority of developing a democratic community.

Finally, the principals were aware of the importance of developing relationships and trust and of being honest when dealing with so many different individuals and perspectives. They listened well and sought to hear all voices. They encouraged and supported the ongoing knowledge and skill development of staff so as to implement new practices. They modeled their shared values, embedded them into their everyday work, and maintained a clear focus and priority on student learning.

SUMMARY

In summary, building democratic community is about respecting difference, and it requires a dedication to open inquiry, commitment to the common good, and recognition of the interdependence of all in achieving this common good. It takes time, listening, caring, and the development of personal regard and relational trust. We believe building democratic community is a factor in improving student learning and needs to be a top priority in any school setting.

Following are a few guiding tips to focus on as you build democratic community:

- Include parents, staff, students, and the surrounding community into your perspective and practices regarding democratic community.
- Set a moral tone for the school that respects difference, listens to all voices, and cares about the common good.

- Create conditions and structures that help staff, parents, and students to work collaboratively with each other and learn from each other.
- Empower staff, parents, and students to share the responsibility for the teaching and learning of all students.

CHAPTER SIX

Building Instructional Program Coherence

How frustrating and difficult is it to accomplish something of substance when you are pulled in several different directions doing unrelated and time-consuming tasks and activities? We are often asked to learn about a variety of curricula, instructional strategies, and assessments and to attend meetings, workshops, and conferences that may not be related to each other and are not consistent with what we are being asked to implement in our schools and classrooms. In addition, some of the school policies about professional development and staff evaluation may actually be barriers that prevent staff from experimenting and implementing new ideas and approaches. We may become further overwhelmed when resources are allocated to unrelated or even contradictory initiatives. To top it off, we may even question the quality of the standards and content we are asking students to learn and apply. Given these conditions, we become pessimistic about the likelihood of advancing achievement for all learners.

This is a common scenario in schools that have not built instructional program coherence. This chapter will begin by defining what we mean by *instructional program coherence*, discuss why such coherence is important, and then return to the stories of our colleagues in Country Elementary School, Bright Lake School, and City High to learn how they built and maintained instructional program coherence.

WHAT IS INSTRUCTIONAL PROGRAM COHERENCE?

Instructional program coherence is defined as "a set of interrelated programs for students and staff that are guided by a common framework for curriculum, instruction, assessment and learning climate and that are pursued over a sustained period" (Newmann, Smith, Allensworth, & Bryk, 2001, p. 297). Strong instructional program coherence is evident when the following conditions are dominant in a school:

1. A common instructional framework guides curriculum, teaching, assessment, and learning climate. The instructional framework means that curriculum, instructional strategies, and assessment of students are coordinated among teachers within a grade level; curriculum and assessments of students proceed logically from one grade level to the next; and student support programs, such as tutoring and parent education, are aligned with the school's instructional framework (Newmann et al., 2001).

2. The working conditions for staff support the implementation of the framework. This includes the expectation that all administrators and staff support and implement the framework and that the school has criteria for recruiting and hiring teachers that is consistent with the framework. In addition, professional development opportunities for staff are consistent with the instructional framework in that that there is an expectation that the skills learned through professional development opportunities will be applied in the classroom (Newmann et al., 2001).

3. The school allocates resources to advance the school's common instructional framework. This includes such things as materials, time, funding, and staff assignments (Newmann et al., 2001).

Instructional program coherence emphasizes the focused and strategic coordination and integration of curriculum, instruction, assessment, student support programs, teaching assignments, teacher performance, professional development, and allocation of resources. Instructional program coherence is actually one way we create an advancing system. All school structures are coordinated and support a common desired end result. The tension between what is wanted by the school staff and community and what their current reality is advances the system as opposed to allowing all involved to become distracted by other demands, initiatives, and interests.

WHY IS INSTRUCTIONAL PROGRAM COHERENCE IMPORTANT?

The primary reason why instructional program coherence is important is that research indicates that it assists student learning (American Psychological Association, 1993; McCombs & Whisler, 1997; Newmann et al., 2002). Students learn and retain more when their learning experiences are connected in a meaningful way to meaningful and relevant work. Students are more likely to put effort into their learning when curricular experiences are connected within classes, among classes, and over time.

In contrast, when students face unrelated learning tasks and activities, they are more likely to approach their learning in a random way with limited focused strategy and less understanding of how they are successful in learning. It is more difficult to understand the content deeply, which leads to a reduction in their motivation and engagement in their learning. Indeed, incoherent activities actually undermine opportunities to gain mastery and the confidence that motivates students to continue their learning (Kanfer, 1990).

Instructional program coherence also supports the teachers' effectiveness. When teachers participate in focused professional development that is sustained over time and is embedded in their work setting, they are more likely to implement the content (Bull & Buechler, 1997). This common focus on the content of teaching and learning can also build community within the school and create a reason for teachers to collaborate and share ideas, and this can impact the quality of their teaching and learning.

Therefore, instructional program coherence is important because it has a positive impact on the learning and effectiveness of both students and teachers. We know schools are more likely to move forward and be successful if the school has a sustained focus; if staff understand and agree on purpose, principles, and goals; if there are common academic standards, curricula, and instruction for all students; if teachers collaborate and assume collective responsibility for all learners; and if there is a consistent culture of high expectations for all students.

Let's now return to the stories of our colleagues in Country Elementary, Bright Lake, and City High to see what they can teach us about their experiences related to instructional program coherence.

COUNTRY ELEMENTARY SCHOOL

As you recall, Country Elementary School made some major adjustments because they were a changing and growing community, there was an increasing percentage of students from poverty, there were low expectations for students in the school, and teachers were exhausted from their effort and confused by their ineffectiveness. They came to a point where this could not continue.

In terms of instructional program coherence, the staff at Country Elementary did not have a common framework or orientation to teaching and learning. Teachers did the best they could do at the time, but their decisions about what and how they taught were essentially made in isolation. There was no coordination within grade levels and certainly no communication about instruction across grade levels. The content of what they taught was driven by the textbooks, and students were passive learners, at best. The teachers felt as if they were really working hard; however, they knew they had no direction and knew they were making no progress with students.

An instructional turning point occurred at a staff meeting when one teacher suggested it might be time for the staff to lower their standards and expectations for their students so they could become more effective in their teaching. When that was said, another staff member spoke up and said, "If we think we should lower the standards, then it is really the time to raise the standards for all students." That was the beginning of their work in relation to instructional program coherence.

The principal recognized the staff needed a common instructional framework, and this became the dominant priority in the school. She realized that she needed to do some personal learning in this area and decided to attend conferences about the various national instructional models and then bring information back and begin to discuss the content with the staff. The staff studied several different national instructional models, and within approximately six months they were leaning toward the Schlechty (2002) working-on-the-work model. One of the reasons this model attracted them was that it provided a clear direction for their work without being overly prescriptive. The Schlechty (2002) model emphasizes the following standards:

- Standard One: Patterns of Engagement
- Standard Two: Student Achievement
- Standard Three: Content and Substance
- Standard Four: Organization of Knowledge
- Standard Five: Product Focus
- Standard Six: Clear and Compelling Products
- Standard Seven: A Safe Environment
- Standard Eight: Affirmation of Performances
- Standard Nine: Affiliation
- Standard Ten: Novelty and Variety
- Standard Eleven: Choice
- Standard Twelve: Authenticity

Principal Joy arranged for various staff members to attend workshops on this model so as to make sure they were extremely clear about what this model advocated. The staff then shared the information with their colleagues, trying to respond to questions and concerns. It became clear that approximately 80% of the staff was supportive of this model, but Principal Joy was not comfortable moving forward until 100% were committed. Therefore, more staff attended professional development workshops and became more familiar with the focus. As a result of all of this, within approximately one year there was unanimous agreement to adopt the Schlechty (2002) model.

The principal worked hard at supporting the staff's learning during this process to make sure they knew exactly what they were committing to and what it meant about their need to change. Their desired end result was essentially that within one to two years, all teachers in Country Elementary would be implementing all 12 standards as described in the model and as evidenced by their actual unit plans, lesson plans, and team notes and observations. They believed this model would assist them in achieving their overarching vision of all students learning with high standards.

When the staff at Country Elementary made this decision, they knew they had a long road ahead, but at least they knew they were going. Their current reality at this time was that all of the teachers had agreed to the model and had received some preliminary training, there was limited time in the schedule for staff to collaborate, there was limited professional development incorporated into the school, and test scores were below the state average.

At this point, they had a clear focus and goal and they knew their current reality, so it was crucial that their action plan would use this tension to move them forward. Now that they had decided on their instructional framework, one of the first action steps was having the principal focus on creating conditions that would allow the staff to learn and apply the model standards. Principal Joy did this in a variety of ways. First, there was ongoing professional development provided by the staff from Schlechty's Center for Leadership in School Reform. In addition, her staff meetings changed from being procedural and business-oriented to focusing on how to apply this instructional framework.

Principal Joy changed the school schedule and created collaborative planning time for staff within grade levels three days a week. She also created an opportunity for staff to apply for a fourth planning time during the week, during which they might work with their colleagues from different grade levels. Furthermore, Principal Joy designed time for floating substitute teachers to release regular teachers from their classrooms in order to meet with her to discuss how the work was progressing and what additional supports the teacher might need. To do this, she needed radically to expand the substitute teacher pool, which she did by training members of the community.

While the principal was continually concerned about students' low test scores, she didn't want to distract the teachers while they were learning and applying their new skills. Therefore, she maintained and analyzed the test data but did not share specific scores or percentages until the end of the year. The scores were definitely important and Principal Joy knew they needed to improve dramatically, but at this point in time she wanted the staff focused on teaching and learning. She knew that staff members were aware of the school's previous low test scores, but she didn't want to use that as their motivator. The teachers needed to learn new skills, to engage students in new ways, and they would deal with test scores in the future.

When looking at Country Elementary's story, it is clear that the principal made some very important moves in creating instructional program coherence. They made a schoolwide decision to adopt the Schlechty (2002) model, which focused and integrated their curriculum, instruction, and assessment. Their professional development was aligned with this model and was provided in an ongoing and embedded manner. Staff meetings were made into learning opportunities. Time was made available for teachers to work together in a consistent manner and to learn from each other. Test scores remained important, but they were not used as the motivator for the school change.

Country Elementary School did transform itself, but as you recall from earlier chapters, it has taken time. What is significant to note here, however, is that within two years of implementing the instructional framework, the state test scores began to rise. Within five years, the state test scores were 10%–20% above the state average. What makes this even more exceptional is that during this time there was an increase in the percentage of students coming from poverty who were enrolled in Country Elementary School. In addition, there was an increase in students with disabilities enrolled in Country Elementary School because they were now being supported in their neighborhood school. Instructional program coherence is obvious now in Country Elementary School, and the results have been nothing less than remarkable.

BRIGHT LAKE SCHOOL

The story of Bright Lake School is quite different from that of Country Elementary School. When Dr. Terry began at Bright Lake

School, there was an already agreed upon learner-centered instructional framework that had been created by a team of teachers in collaboration with the school board, but broad-based support had not yet been established. It was up to the principal to take this instructional framework to scale to all of the teams across the school and build instructional program coherence.

The learner-centered instructional framework was based on the following assumptions:

- All students can learn everything we feel it is important for them to know.
- We can create schools where learning is a constant and time a variable.
- Families of learners involve parents, students, and other significant adults in determining learning goals.
- Technology will enhance learning opportunities for all students.
- Innovation is an ongoing process.

The instructional framework included the following elements for all students:

- Creative and critical thinking
- Communication
- Collaboration and social responsibility
- Independent functioning

When Dr. Terry began, only one team out of nine understood the framework and was well on the road to applying and implementing the strategies and goals. The current reality at this point in time was that the various teams were functioning differently from each other, not all the teams were comfortable with the instructional framework, there was strong school board support for this instructional framework, there had been minimal professional development about the instructional framework, the school's test scores were average with plenty of room for growth, and community support was polarized.

Given the variability among the teams, the principal developed an action plan that built capacity differently, team by team, based on their needs. She offered a nine-month planning process for

Build capacity one by one

each team interested in moving forward with the framework. She provided professional development for a semester and throughout the summer. She created a new structure, the Program Council, composed of Bright Lake teachers. The council's function was to assist in unifying the teams while developing and applying the instructional framework across all teams. In terms of the assessment process, Dr. Terry took a lead role in working with some of the staff to develop an assessment plan that was aligned with the standards.

Dr. Terry clearly created new structures and conditions that allowed the teams the opportunity to learn and apply their new skills and knowledge related to learner-centered principles and practices. She used the available resources in terms of time and materials in ways that were supportive of the overall goals of the instructional framework and kept the teams focused on learning what they needed to learn. If the teams began to talk about the difficulty of doing this work or made excuses for why they couldn't do this work, she listened to them and then refocused the conversation to what they were trying to achieve with this instructional framework. She would not lose sight of the overall goal of the instructional framework and of achieving instructional program coherence.

Within four years, all but one team were involved with implementing all of the practices of the learner-centered instructional framework. Bright Lake did not experience low test scores prior to implementing the learner-centered instructional framework. However, once the learner-centered practices were implemented throughout the school, test scores indicated that the students involved in the learner-centered instructional framework early on achieved higher scores than the students who were in the more traditional, teacher-directed classrooms. As student scores showed high performance, community polarization about the learner-centered teams settled down into more generalized support for the instructional framework.

Instructional program coherence was created in Bright Lake and the impact on student learning was clear. The principal made the direction of the school clear, provided ongoing support, created structures to support the work, allocated resources in support of the work, and created an overall assessment plan that documented the results.

CITY HIGH SCHOOL

High schools are typically structured with separate departments and limited, if any, instructional coherence occurs. What is unusual about the City High School story is how instructional coherence is beginning to occur in such a large, typical high school.

Principal John recognized the impact of not having instructional coherence at City High after he attended a conference at which two national presenters discussed the importance of using data-driven decision making. Principal John observed a lack of consistency regarding what was being assessed in the various departments at City High School. He realized that if there wasn't a common view on what was being assessed, there also wasn't consistency regarding what was being taught.

With this insight, he talked to the department chairs and suggested the need to establish common rubrics for all introductory chemistry courses. The department chairs created an ad hoc committee to create the rubrics. The rubrics were developed and implemented in all of the introductory chemistry courses in one year. This created further discussion among the teachers about what content they were teaching as well as what pedagogy they used. In this story, instructional program coherence began by determining what assessments would be used across one department.

Because there was an emphasis on writing in the state assessment, Principal John and the staff suggested that writing would be the next area in which they would establish a common set of rubrics. Principal John followed the same process as with the chemistry courses by establishing an ad hoc team of teachers to develop the rubrics and share them with their colleagues for feedback and implementation.

Principal John was responsible for identifying the area of concern, communicating it, and establishing structures by which teachers could collaborate and get the rubrics developed. He made it a priority and provided the necessary time, and the work was completed and implemented within the department. Considering the separate structures in typical high schools, this is an impressive example of figuring out how to work with the given structure, understanding the forces at play, and creating a desired end result.

LESSONS LEARNED FROM OUR STORIES

Although the stories of these three schools are quite different, there are some common themes and lessons. Although the principals certainly viewed the need for an identified instructional framework as a priority, none of the principals took it upon themselves to select the framework and impose it on the staff. The principal of Country Elementary had involvement of all of the staff in selecting the model. The principal of Bright Lake inherited an instructional framework that had been created by a team of teachers in collaboration with the school board, but without broad-based support. The principal of City High School suggested rubrics be developed, but did not dictate the criteria or content. All of the principals saw the need to have a common approach to instruction and assessment, believed it would assist in student learning, and engaged the staff in understanding this priority.

The Country Elementary and Bright Lake principals provided ongoing and embedded professional development that supported the implementation of the instructional framework. All three principals provided teachers with the time to work and learn together so as to apply their new knowledge and get their work implemented. All of the principals used the existing resources to support the instructional framework or assessment framework and did not bombard the staff with random activities and initiatives that would distract them from their work.

The Country Elementary and Bright Lake principals were also highly concerned about not only having coherence in the instructional framework but also making sure the students were engaged in worthwhile work. Both schools were building the capacity of teachers to challenge students with high learning standards while engaging them in authentic work and valuing the student voice in the learning process.

Finally, all of the principals had deliberate plans to move the work forward. They knew where they wanted to go, they knew what was going to help and hinder their efforts, and they strategically put professional development plans and structures for learning in place. They made changes in the plans when necessary but did not get distracted by other demands.

SUMMARY

In summary, we have learned that instructional program coherence is essential in any whole-school reform effort. There needs to be an explicit instructional framework that connects curriculum, instruction, and assessment practices. Professional development needs to be provided in an ongoing and embedded manner that supports the instructional framework. In addition, resources need to be allocated to support the work, and policies and structures also need to be designed to allow staff to learn and apply their new knowledge and skills.

Following are a few guiding tips as you think about promoting instructional program coherence in your school:

- Ensure that instructional program coherence is focused on worthwhile educational goals.
- Be careful of any instructional frameworks that are so prescriptive that they stifle professional expertise or inhibit staff from raising legitimate questions or concerns.
- Recognize ongoing professional development, collaboration, community, and common planning time as critical elements in taking an instructional framework to scale within a school.
- Recognize and eliminate any distractions and random initiatives that would redirect the teachers' focus and energy and keep the goals of the instructional framework clear and sustained.
- Be deliberate in your planning and your support for building instructional program coherence.

CHAPTER SEVEN

Advancing the Work of Leaders

W hat did the principals of Country Elementary, Bright Lake, and City High schools do to transform their schools? What were the key elements of their leadership that advanced their work? How did they keep the work focused over so many years? Why was this so important to them? In this chapter, we discuss some specific elements and demands about leadership and what this means for you in your day-to-day work.

ELEMENTS OF LEADERSHIP

While a great deal has been written in the literature about leadership, our purpose in this section is not to review this content but to identify some elements from structural dynamics suggesting critical actions that leaders can take to move systems forward. Though many of these ideas have been mentioned in the previous chapters and stories, we bring them together now to provide direction for your work.

Clarity

To begin, there must be clarity of vision, purpose, and principles. Clarity provides direction, helps people know what there is to do and why it is important to do it, and helps people know how to support the organization's vision and values by translating them into action (Fritz, 1996). Such clarity is no doubt difficult to achieve, given the many demands made on schools and teachers. However, it is essential to be descriptive and honest when working with staff, parents, community, and students about the vision for the school. We need to stay away from jargon and clichés that may sound good for the moment but do little to help people understand what it is we are actually talking about doing.

Recall from our stories that the work at Country Elementary School did not begin with clarity about the specific changes needed. Clarity emerged as the principal, staff, and parents had an ongoing dialogue about the need to change expectations for all students. Clarity also emerged at City High School when it became apparent to the principal that not all students were learning to high levels and that all school resources were not available to all students. Bright Lake School, in contrast, had clarity of vision within one team, which then had to be translated to the other teams in the school. You need to be able to talk about the vision clearly so that others can understand and question the ideas. Clarity of vision, purpose, and principles may not happen as quickly as we would like, but it does need to happen.

Priorities

Priorities and choices need to be related to the overall vision. We need to make distinctions about what is more and what is less important and decide what gets done at different points in time. If we don't prioritize and make some choices, then everything is of equal importance and it becomes too overwhelming to develop plans for any of the work, and so nothing gets done. To choose everything is to do nothing. It is often difficult to prioritize our work in schools when everything seems equally important. However, we must think about what matters most, what makes sense to prioritize, and we must continually remember that this type of work is ongoing: It takes many years to bring about large-scale change.

Recall in our stories about Country Elementary School how the principal continually had to prioritize and make choices about the nature and focus of their work. Even though the principal knew they needed to change expectations for students, establish relationships with parents, establish an instructional framework, and create a learning community, she certainly knew they couldn't do it all at once. They needed to set some priorities, be clear about the focus, and then support it in multiple ways. Note that while some areas were being focused on, the principal was preparing for the next set of priorities to take center stage. So, it's not as if *every-thing* else had to be put on hold until the current work is completely accomplished. The principal of Country Elementary kept close tabs on how the work was progressing and was deliberate about when to begin the next phase.

This was also the case at City High School. When the principal and staff had more clarity about the achievement gap and that all students did not have access to the school's resources, the priorities became apparent. There was a concentrated focus on improving learning for students who were not achieving and on providing access to all school supports and services for all students. These became the school's priorities, and decisions were made with these issues in mind.

Professional Development

To bring about change, there also must be an emphasis on professional development. If schools have people who can learn, then schools can transform themselves. If schools don't have people who can learn, those schools can't change in any meaningful way. We need to create schools in which learning is everyone's job, because learning is frequently required to achieve the desired end results.

Just recall all of the professional development that was provided and learning that had to occur at Country Elementary School on the part of the principal, staff, parents, and students. Professional development and learning were essential parts of ultimately producing the remarkable student achievement.

Learning should not be viewed as an activity that occurs once in awhile, but rather as an orientation (Fritz, 1996). A learning orientation means that individuals are encouraged to learn from their mistakes, experimentation is valued, and it is understood that new ideas and projects generally begin with flaws and that correction and adjustment are parts of the learning process.

Recall the story of Bright Lake School, where the principal established ongoing cycles of professional development for teams to learn about the instructional framework. These cycles were established for nine months and extended into the summer months as well. In addition, recall how Country Elementary School had several teams initially learn about their instructional framework and had ongoing internal and external support to implement the practices. Learning became a part of the way the school functioned and was absolutely necessary for the work to move forward in these schools.

The professional development at City High School began with building the knowledge and skills of the teachers who worked with minority students. There was also a focus on creating common assessments and rubrics in academic departments so as to hold high standards and expectations for all students. Professional development was aligned with the priority of improving learning for students who were not achieving.

Everything these principals did related to learning, not just the learning of students but also to the learning of the adults in the schools. Their orientation was always focused on directing their professional development resources to build staff capacity to move toward implementing those key practices deemed essential to realizing their vision.

Democratic Community

Finally, creating a democratic community where there is a common purpose as well as respect for difference is essential for change to occur. A democratic community includes and welcomes staff, student, parents, and the surrounding community into the life of the school. A democratic community can help provide a framework for what to do, why to do it, how to do it, and how to be critical and raise questions and concerns. A democratic community supports inquiry, dialogue, and critique, while promoting care and concern for the common good, trust, respect, and equity.

The principal and staff at Country Elementary School decided to have high expectations for all students, to seek out parents' voices in school decisions, to gain parent trust, and to work collaboratively. The principal created conditions for this to happen by changing the school schedule so staff could collaborate, by meeting with parents at times and places where the parents were comfortable, and by changing the focus of staff meetings to be about teaching and learning.

The principal of Bright Lake needed to gain support from school-based teams as well as the community regarding the learning-centered instructional framework. She developed a Program Council featuring staff representatives to work through issues related to the vision and practices. In addition, she created the Families as Partners Council made up of parents from the different houses in the school in order for them to have a voice in the newly developing vision and practices. The Bright Lake principal also created conditions throughout the years for staff to meet with each other, learn from each other, and create trusting relationships with the students and families.

We believe these four elements—having clarity of vision, establishing priorities, providing professional development, and creating community—are vital elements for leaders who will be successful in creating advancing systems for moving schools forward.

DEMANDS OF LEADERSHIP

In order to have clarity of vision, establish priorities with thoughtfulness, support meaningful professional development and learning, and create community, we believe there are four demands that leaders must meet to do the kind of work described in these chapters. These leadership demands are based on the work of William Foster (1989) and should guide your overall thinking and practice of leadership.

Be Critical

The first demand is that leadership must be critical. We need to continually question and critique our work and examine all aspects of a situation to assure all perspectives and voices are understood. We need continually to examine if there are ways to improve the human condition for all individuals and not accept lower standards for some. We need to make sure we are asking the right questions and not avoiding learning what we may be afraid of uncovering. We need to question our understandings of reality and continually work toward practices that will result in improvements for all.

The principal of Country Elementary School demonstrated leadership that was critical by asking how they could raise expectations for all students. It was not acceptable to have lower expectations for some students and not prepare them adequately for the future. The principal of Bright Lake School demonstrated leadership that was critical by expecting all teams to implement the instructional framework and thereby enhance the quality of education for all students.

The principal of City High School was horrified when he learned that students with disabilities were typically excluded from various activities in the high school. He examined this practice, asked questions, determined it was not acceptable, and made immediate changes. He demonstrated leadership that was critical by uncovering an unfair practice and making changes that would benefit all. All principals studied in our stories demonstrated leadership that was critical.

Be Transformative

The second demand is that leadership must be transformative. Leadership must be oriented toward social change (Foster, 1989). Transformation is not a special or unique occurrence. Rather, it happens in everyday events when leaders take a stand and exert some effect on their situations. The social change we speak of does not necessarily mean societal change: Social change can be accomplished without the complete and total restructuring of any given society. Social change occurs frequently, in small doses, through the actions and activities of various groups and individuals who hope to make some sort of difference.

Our stories clearly speak of transformative leadership. The Country Elementary School principal, staff, and parents ultimately decided to transform their school so that all students had an equitable education with equal educational opportunities. They were leveling the playing field so that all students could have choices about their future and not automatically be relegated to future low-paying jobs. This would clearly create social change.

The Bright Lake principal did not think it appropriate for only a small number of students to have access to the more authentic and engaging curriculum offered by the leading-edge teams. In the long run, the principal recognized this type of learner-centered curriculum would better prepare students for their futures, and she didn't accept that some students would not have this experience.

The City High School principal did not accept that some students were being excluded from different activities in the high school and community. He clearly wanted to provide equal access for all students, which could lead to social change in the larger sense. All three of our principals demonstrated leadership that was transformative.

Be Educative

The third demand is that leadership is educative. What we mean by this is that a leader can present both a vision and an analysis. Being educative means envisioning a new future as well as analyzing the current situation. The vision has to do with what is desired and how new social arrangements can be designed. The analysis has to do with understanding the reality of the situation and engaging in self-reflection. The combined effect of vision and analysis is to raise everyone's awareness of the projected future as well as the current reality simultaneously.

All three principals in our stories demonstrated leadership that was educative. The principal of Country Elementary School and her staff were creating a vision of a new future while they were uncovering their current reality. From this, they figured out what they needed to learn and do. The principal of Bright Lake School also had a new vision and knew the teams were in different stages of development. An action plan to implement the instructional framework with all teams was designed based on this understanding.

The principal of City High School had a vision that African American males could achieve in all areas, used data to uncover the achievement gap, and then created a cohort plan for these students with the school and community. The educative aspect of leadership should push people to begin to question their previous ways of working, to grow and develop because of this questioning, and to begin to consider alternative ways of ordering their work.

Be Ethical

The fourth demand is for leadership to be ethical. Leadership in general must maintain an ethical focus that is oriented toward democratic values within a community. We believe leadership carries a responsibility not only to be personally moral but also to make an ethical commitment to the community in which one lives and works.

Again, the principals in our stories demonstrated leadership that was ethical. The Country Lake School principal and staff decided their work would not be ethical if all students were not held to similar standards. The Bright Lake School principal was committed to providing an instructional framework that was engaging and promoted self-responsible learning for all students, not just some. The City High School principal made a clear choice to include all students in all school activities and explicitly focus on closing the achievement gap that was evident with African American males.

These four leadership demands should help guide your thinking and practice about your work as leaders. Leadership, in the final analysis, is the ability to relate deeply to each other to create a more desired future. Leadership is a consensual task in which there is a sharing of ideas and responsibilities and an overarching commitment to improving the social conditions for all people.

CREATING GREAT SCHOOLS

These elements and demands for leadership provide the focus for your work. However, it is also important to consider how your school will continue to transform without relying only on you, the identified leader in the school. This section will briefly highlight some additional points about organizations that will help maximize your leadership success and the future success of the school.

Leadership and power need to be distributed throughout the school and community in order to transform your school. As you already know, you cannot do this work alone. You need to build connections and relationships and to distribute leadership and power in places where they are needed.

Each of the three principals in our stories distributed leadership and power. The Country Elementary School principal wanted parents to recognize their own power by meeting with them on their own terms in a place in which they were comfortable. Throughout the work at Country Elementary, staff and parents learned they were all responsible for all students and all assumed a leadership role at various points in time. The Bright Lake School principal shared leadership and power by creating a council comprised of teachers that served as a keeper of the vision. The principal of City High School developed cohorts of teachers and department chairs to share responsibility for the initiative to increase the achievement of African American males. You need to find ways to distribute leadership and power so the work becomes shared and all students become everyone's responsibility.

You also need to build an infrastructure of policies that are aligned with and in support of your overall vision, principles, and purpose. These policies need to be fair to all, consistently applied, and supportive of growth and development. The three principals in our stories effectively built an infrastructure of policy support. Both Country Elementary School and Bright Lake School principals created a supportive policy for teachers to have time to meet, learn, and plan together. There were specific cycles of professional development at Bright Lake School for teams that were beginning to implement the new instructional framework. Policy that supports the work is necessary for staff to continue to implement new ideas in the future, even when staff and leaders change.

Finally, resources, in terms of money, ideas, materials, and people, need to be aligned with the overall purposes of the work, and you need to be deliberate when deciding what types of activities should be supported. We need to support what we are working on and not lose direction by fragmenting the limited available resources. All three principals from our stories allocated their available resources to specifically support their work.

SUMMARY

We hope our stories highlight how these principals, parents, students, and communities transformed their schools. We hope you will begin to see things within a structural perspective, understand why certain things are simply bound to happen, and know how to build new structures to change course, when necessary. Your work is not about solving problems but about creating what you want to bring into being—what really matters most to you.

We also hope you now know your work is about creating social change, envisioning desired futures, and uncovering current reality. This work requires knowing how to create a plan to move the work forward with a focus on democratic community and instructional program coherence. This work takes heart, mind, and soul, and we wish you much thoughtfulness, stamina, spirit, and success during your journey. As we said in our Acknowledgements, we congratulate those who persist in the work of leadership.

References

American Psychological Association. (1993). *Learner-centered psychological principles: Guidelines for school redesign and reform.* Washington, DC: American Psychological Association and Mid-Continent Regional Educational Laboratory.

American Psychological Association, Work Group of the Board of Educational Affairs. (1997). *Learner-centered psychological principles: A framework for school reform and redesign.* Washington, DC: American Psychological Association.

Bryk, A., Lee, V., & Holland, P. (1993). *Catholic schools and the common good.* Cambridge, MA: Harvard University Press.

Bryk, A., & Schneider, B. (2003). Trust in schools: A core resource for school reform. *Educational Leadership, 60*(6), 40–45.

Bull, B., & Buechler, M. (1997). *Planning together: Professional development for teachers of all students.* Bloomington: Indiana Education Policy Center.

Collins, J., & Porras, J. (1996, September/October). Building your company's vision. *Harvard Business Review,* pp. 65–77.

Comer, J. P., Haynes, N. M., Joyner, E. T., & Ben-Avie, M. (1996). *Rallying the whole village: The Comer process for reforming education.* New York: Teachers College Press.

Foster, W. (1989). Toward a critical practice of leadership. In J. Smyth (Ed.), *Critical perspectives on educational leadership* (pp. 39–62). London: Falmer.

Fritz, R. (1996). *Corporate tides: The inescapable laws of organizational structure.* San Francisco: Berrett-Koehler.

Fritz, R. (1999). *Path of least resistance for managers: Designing organizations to succeed.* San Francisco: Berrett-Koehler.

Furman, G., & Starratt, J. (2002). Leadership for democratic community in schools. In J. Murphy (Ed.), *The educational leadership challenge: Redefining leadership for the 21st century* (pp. 105–133). Chicago: The University of Chicago Press.

Gladwell, M. (2000). *The tipping point: How little things can make a big difference.* Boston: Little, Brown.

Kanfer, R. (1990). Motivation theory and industrial and organization psychology. In M. D. Dunnette & L. M. Hough (Eds.), *Handbook of industrial and organizational psychology* (2nd ed., Vol. 1, pp. 75–170). Palo Alto, CA: Psychologists Press.

Louis, K. S., & Kruse, S. D. (1995). *Professionalism and community: Perspectives on reforming urban schools.* Thousand Oaks, CA: Corwin Press.

McCombs, B., & Whisler, J. S. (1997). *The learner-centered classroom and school: Strategies for increasing student motivation and achievement.* San Francisco: Jossey-Bass.

Meier, D. (1995). *The power of their ideas: Lessons for America from a small school in Harlem.* Boston: Beacon.

Newmann, F., Smith, B. A., Allensworth, E., & Bryk, A. (2001). Instructional program coherence: What it is and why it should guide school improvement policy. *Educational Evaluation and Policy Analysis, 23*(4), 297–321.

Postman, N. (1996). *The end of education: Redefining the value of school.* New York: Vintage.

Schlechty, P. (1997). *Inventing better schools: An action plan for educational reform.* San Francisco: Jossey-Bass.

Schlechty, P. (2002). *Working on the work: An action plan for teachers, principals, and superintendents.* San Francisco: Jossey-Bass.

Glossary

Advancing Structure: the creative process, wherein something is created and then, because it was created, supports more and more future creations (Fritz, 1999, p. 17).

Core Values: the essential and enduring tenets of an organization or school that are in support and pursuit of the purpose (Collins & Porras, 1996).

Democratic Community: a "community of difference," in which "difference is celebrated but interdependence is recognized, and the common good, locally and globally, is the glue" (Furman & Starratt, 2002, p. 116).

Instructional Program Coherence: "a set of interrelated programs for students and staff that are guided by a common framework for curriculum, instruction, assessment and learning climate and that are pursued over a sustained period" (Newmann, Smith, Allensworth, & Bryk, 2001, p. 297).

Leadership Demands: items defined in terms of being (1) critical—continually examining if there are ways to improve the human condition for all individuals and not accept lower standards for some; (2) transformative—orienting the work of leaders toward social change; (3) educative—envisioning a new future as well as analyzing the current situation; and (4) ethical—maintaining an ethical focus that is oriented toward democratic values within a community (Foster, 1989).

Oscillating Structure: "the path of least resistance . . . [that] moves from one place to another, but then moves back toward its original position. A period of advancement is followed by a reversal. Success and progress are nullified" (Fritz, 1999, p. 18).

Principles: an organization's core values (Collins & Porras, 1996).

Purpose: an organization's "reason for being." It is people's idealistic motivations for doing the work and is the organization's foundation (Collins & Porras, 1996).

Shift of Dominance: an aspect of structural conflict; movement between one tension-resolution system and its competing tension-resolution system. A shift of dominance produces a predictable oscillating pattern, as the path of least resistance moves first from one type of action (e.g., eating) to another (e.g., dieting).

Structural Conflict: two competing tension-resolution systems based on two competing goals.

Structural Dynamics: a study of how structures work, through analysis of how elements combine to produce predictable patterns of behavior.

Structural Tension: the difference between what you have right now and what you want; the difference between the goal/end result and the current reality/current state.

Structural Tension Chart: a planning tool with end results at the top, the current reality at the bottom, and action steps in the middle.

Structure: an entity made up of individual elements that have an impact upon one another by the relationships they form (Fritz, 1999, p. 25).

Systems Dynamics: a study of how systems work, through an analysis of feedback loops.

Tension-Resolution System: one end result (goal) and its connected current reality.

Tolerable Conflict: mutually exclusive goals exist and cancel out each other's ultimate success, though each goal may be achieved to some extent.

Index

**CORWIN
PRESS**

The Corwin Press logo—a raven striding across an open book—represents
the union of courage and learning. Corwin Press is committed to improving
education for all learners by publishing books and other professional
development resources for those serving the field of K–12 education. By
providing practical, hands-on materials, Corwin Press continues to carry out
the promise of its motto: **"Helping Educators Do Their Work Better."**